CAST IRON
COOKBOOK FOR BEGINNERS 2022

1200 Days of Easy, Fresh, and Healthy Pan Recipes for Your Cast Iron Skillet and Dutch Oven

Patric Stoner

Table of Contents

Introduction

What Is a Cast Iron Skillet?

Cast iron is one of the oldest cooking materials. It has been used for decades due to its valued heat retention. A cast-iron skillet takes the shape of a grill pan or frying pan but is made completely of cast iron. This creates a heavy, durable, and sturdy cooking vessel that can cook just about anything inside of it.

Benefits of Cast Iron

Cast Iron Skillets Get Better with Age

One of its greatest advantages is that a cast-iron pan is the only piece of kitchen gear you can buy, that improves after years of hard use. As you cook in it, a cast-iron pan progressively develops a natural patina, called seasoning, which releases food easily.

It Maintains Heat

Cast iron doesn't heat very evenly because its thermal conductivity, or ability to transfer heat from one part of the metal to another, is very low. What cast iron does do well is hold on to heat: Once cast iron cookware gets completely hot, it will stay hot. This makes cast iron the ideal material for high-heat applications like searing steak. The initial drop in temperature caused by adding the relatively low- temperature steak to the hot skillet will be much smaller in cast iron, allowing for higher heat and better browning. This makes for a more even and desirable result for foods like meats and steaks.

Cast Iron is Extremely Durable

Cast iron is truly the stuff of legend, many people are still cooking on cast-iron pans handed down through their families for generations. They are virtually indestructible and only get better with every use.

It Can Develop A Nonstick Coating

Cast iron's ability to develop a nonstick coating also makes it incredibly versatile. This is a boon for minimalist cooks who are looking to downsize their pot and pan collections to a few key pieces that can work in almost any application, but cast iron is also beloved by gourmet cooks who appreciate the particular benefits it offers for essential techniques like browning and searing.

Considerations For Using Cast Iron Skillets

In the beginning, a cast iron can be a major adjustment for chefs. These pans are not the best right out of the gate. They require some time and a few uses to get where they need to be to create great foods. The size and weight can also be another challenge for chefs that are used to handling modern cookware. Cast iron is extremely heavy and can make handling a bit more difficult when you need quick and easy movement. As mentioned before, cast iron has poor thermal conductivity, which can be another challenge to get used to. Typically, you can cook right when a pan hits the heat, but with cast iron, it requires preheating to get the best results.

How to Clean Cast Iron Skillets

Cleaning cast iron skillets is something that modern chefs can have a hard time coming to terms with at first. Cleaning cast iron is, unlike any other cookware. You can clean cast iron when it is still hot without ruining the integrity of the pan, but water can be a cast-iron skillet's worst nightmare. Leaving them in the sink or water can ruin them in a heartbeat. Wash them as soon as you are finished cooking and dry them immediately.

To make sure your cast iron skillet provides you with all of the benefits listed above, it needs to be seasoned. This is a process that is completed after washing. The seasoning on the pan requires a bit of oil. To season a cast-iron skillet, dip a paper towel into coconut oil or any oil of your choosing and rub the inside of the hot pan. Make sure that you are safe when you complete this and that your hands do not come in contact with the surface. Rub-down the surface with the oiled cloth and then store the pan in a dry place.

Cast Iron Equipment

1. Lodge Cast Iron Baking Pan

Since it absorbs and maintains heat so well, cast iron is the ideal material for creating good pizza crust, which requires searingly hot temperatures. While a baking stone takes an hour to reach 500 degrees, this pan by Lodge was ready after a mere 30 minutes and retained the heat as we baked four pizzas in a row. Pizza baked up perfectly and the pan's looped handles made it easy to move in and out of the oven.

2. Nordic Ware Cast Aluminum Stovetop Belgian Waffler

This waffle iron was ready to use out of the box, heated up evenly and quickly, and made golden brown, crisp waffles that released easily. Easy-to-follow instructions and thin, flat handles facilitated perfect waffle-making on electric stoves. A quick scrub and rinse were all that was needed to clean the nonstick metal.

3. Imusa Cast Iron Tortilla Press

This product is lighter and more compact than a heavy wooden tortilladora but still has sufficient heft to make pressing easy. The handle arrives detached, so there is some assembly required (though the instructions are clear and easy to follow). At first, the handle was a bit stiff, but it loosened with use, and the ample surface area kept the dough from squeezing out the sides.

4. Lodge 12-inch Tempered Glass Cover

This lightweight lid helped produce nicely browned onions and evenly cooked eggs, and it was much easier to lift and clean than the heavy cast-iron lid. It contained moisture and messes, and its glass material allowed users to get a good sense of how their food was cooking.

5. Knapp Made Small Ring CM Scrubber

The Small Ring Scrubber effortlessly removed cooked-on bacon and hamburger from cast iron and lasagna from our 13 by 9-inch baking dish. This scrubber's larger size allowed it to cover more area efficiently, and we especially appreciated its fine rings, which scoured narrow grill pan grooves with ease. The smaller rings did, however, make this scrubber harder to clean. We don't recommend using either scrubber on enamelware or stainless steel.

6. OXO Good Grips Silicone Pot Holder With Magnet

Whatever we were maneuvering including a screaming-hot skillet, we always felt safe and confident using this potholder. It had cotton for flexibility and comfort and grippy, high-heat silicone for protection. At 10 by 8 inches, it was big enough for full coverage but also nimble, thanks to a pocket that allowed testers to precisely pinch thin baking sheet rims and to rotate cake pans with ease.

How to Season a Cast Iron Skillet

To get a well-seasoned pan, essentially, you have to oil the inside of the cooking surface and then heat it until the fat polymerizes, repeating the process to build up a protective layer.

Here we describe in detail the steps to follow:

Step 1: Wash out the pan

You may have heard that you should never ever use soap on cast iron. That's not entirely true—a well-seasoned skillet has enough of a coating that a little surfactant won't hurt it. Still, in general, plain water is the way to go—unless you're about to reseason the pan.

In this case, you want to get rid of any little food particles and bits of rust on the surface before you season, so you can create the smoothest possible coating. That means you should use soap. If your pan is rusted out, take some steel wool to it and scrub that red color off. Really go for it, and feel free to scour the outside of the pan as well—it can't hurt.

Step 2: Dry thoroughly

Dry the skillet with a paper towel, and if you want to be really thorough, pop it on the stove over low heat to evaporate any residual water molecules. Again, you'll want to create a smooth layer of oil, and any lingering water droplets will interrupt that process.

Step 3: Rub it with oil

Canola oil is a standard go-to for seasoning. Vegetable oil and corn oil both work fine, too. Technically, any oil or fat should do the trick, but the aforementioned are better than others because they can get pretty hot before they start smoking. You're going to heat your pan to over 400°F, so any fat with a low smoke point will fill your oven (and house) with haze. Solid fats like shortening also have high smoke points, but they're harder to smear over the pan in a thin, even layer, so you should stick to liquids.

Smear the oil on the metal with a paper towel, keeping in mind that you only need a patina of fat. Make sure to coat the whole surface, inside and out. Rub it all in until it no longer looks greasy. If you leave too much fat on the cast iron, it'll form pools, and you'll end up with hardened droplets of polymerized oil in your pan.

Step 4: Heat the whole pan in the oven

Next, you need to expose the whole pan to a nice even heat, so you can't just plop it on a stovetop. Put it in a 450°F oven, upside down, with another pan beneath it in case it drips. Leave it for half an hour.

At this point, some experts advise you to turn off the oven and leave the pan in there to cool. Others suggest repeating the oiling and heating process a few more times—three or four, in total—to bake on a really solid layer of fat. The latter method works better, especially if you've really wrecked your pan.

So, take the pan out, and rub a bit more oil into the iron. Pop it back in the oven for 30 minutes. Repeat.

BREAKFAST RECIPES

1. Cowboy Breakfast Skillet

Cook Time: 10 mins Total Time: 10 mins Servings: 4

Ingredients

- 1 - 4.2 oz. Box dry hashbrowns
- 1/2 cup diced green pepper chop
- 1/2 cup diced onion chop
- 1 cup shredded cheese
- 6 eggs
- 6 pre-cooked turkey sausage links broken into pieces
- 1 tbsp. Olive oil
- Salt and pepper to taste

Instructions

1. Add water to hashbrowns per box instructions.
2. Heat oil in the skillet.
3. Add onions, green peppers, and sausage. Saute until veggies are translucent.
4. Add hydrated hashbrowns and let cook for 5 minutes, flipping occasionally.
5. Clear a space in the middle of the hashbrowns and add eggs.
6. Gently stir until eggs are cooked through.
7. Top with cheese. Turn heat off and cover.
8. Serve once the cheese has melted

Nutritional Value

Calories: 344kcal | Carbohydrates: 18g | Protein: 18g | Fat: 22g | Saturated Fat: 7g

2. Cast Iron Breakfast Skillet Recipe

Prep Time: 10 minutes Cook Time: 30 minutes

Total Time: 40 minutes Servings: 6

Ingredients

- 3 cups frozen shredded hash browns
- 3 tbsp vegetable oil divided
- 1 green bell pepper small, chopped and seeded
- 1 onion finely chopped
- 1 garlic clove finely chopped
- 4 oz mushrooms sliced
- 1 tsp kosher salt divided
- 1/4 cup ripe black olives sliced
- 1/4 cup sun-dried tomatoes in oil drained and chopped
- 6 large eggs lightly whisked
- 1/4 tsp ground black pepper
- 4 oz mozzarella cheese shredded

Instructions

1. Preheat oven to 350 degrees F.
2. Place a cast iron or non-stick oven-safe skillet over medium heat. Add oil, bell pepper, onion, and mushrooms and cook for 3-5 minutes, stirring occasionally. Add garlic and cook for 30 seconds.
3. Pour in the hash browns and 1/2 tsp. of salt and stir to combine with the bell pepper and mushrooms. Spread out the hash browns in an even layer. Add another Tbsp of oil and cook 5-7 minutes without stirring.
4. Use a pancake-turner and carefully turn the hash browns over. Press down if necessary, to form an even layer.
5. Cook another 4-6 minutes without stirring or until the hash browns are a golden brown. Remove from the heat and set aside.
6. While the hash browns cook, combine the eggs, olives, sun-dried tomatoes, pepper, 1/2 tsp. of salt, pepper, and shredded cheese in a bowl and whisk to combine.
7. Pour the egg mixture evenly over the hash brown layer in the skillet.
8. Bake for 9-10 minutes or until the eggs are set.
9. Cut into wedges and serve immediately.

Nutritional Value

Calories: 233kcal | Carbohydrates: 23g | Protein: 9g | Fat: 12g |

3. Cowboy Breakfast Skillet (Alternative version)

Prep Time: 5 minutes Cook Time: 30 minutes

Total Time: 35 minutes Servings: 5

Ingredients

- 7 strips bacon about 1/2 pound
- 4 cups frozen cubed hash brown potatoes
- 1 teaspoon salt
- 1/4 tsp. pepper
- 5 eggs
- 3/4 cup shredded Cheddar cheese
- 3 Tbsp butter

Instructions

1. In a large skillet cook bacon until crisp over medium heat. Remove bacon, but keep 2 – 3 Tbsp of bacon drippings in the skillet. Crumble bacon and set aside.
2. Add potatoes, salt, and pepper to the drippings in the skillet, cook and stir for 2 minutes over medium heat.
3. Cover and cook, stirring occasionally until potatoes are browned and tender, about 12 – 15 minutes. About 10 minutes into this time add 1 Tbsp of butter at a time where the skillet is dry as needed.
4. Make 5 wells in the potato mixture. Break one egg in each well. Cover and cook on low heat for 8 to 10 minutes or until eggs are completely set.
5. Sprinkle with shredded cheese and crumbled bacon and serve warm right out of the skillet.

Nutritional Value

Calories: 458kcal | Carbohydrates: 31g | Protein: 17g | Fat: 30g

4. Farmers Breakfast Skillet

Prep Time: 25 mins Cook Time: 20 mins

Total Time: 45 mins Servings: 12

Ingredients

- ½ Lb bacon
- 1 20 oz package refrigerated shredded hash browns
- 4 medium green onion sliced
- ½ medium red bell pepper diced
- ½ medium green bell pepper diced
- 8 oz cubed ham or cooked sausage
- 12 large eggs
- ½ cup half & half or heavy cream
- 1 ½ cup shredded cheese your preference
- Seasoned salt and black pepper to taste

Instructions

1. Preheat the oven to 350°F. On cast-iron, cook the bacon until crisp. Remove from the skillet to paper towels to drain, reserving the drippings in the pan.
2. Add the green onion and sliced bell peppers to the drippings. Reserve some of the green onion for garnishing.
3. Saute over medium-high for 3 minutes or until softened. Season with seasoned salt and black pepper to your taste.
4. Add the shredded hash brown potatoes to the pan. Cook for 6-8 minutes, stirring periodically until lightly browned and heated through. Season with a sprinkle of seasoned salt and black pepper.
5. Spread the hash browns evenly on the bottom of the skillet, then sprinkle the crumbled bacon and cubed ham over the hash browns.
6. Top with ½ of the shredded cheese. Reserve some bacon for garnishing.
7. Whip the eggs or egg whites with half & half or cream. Season lightly with seasoned salt and black pepper. Pour on top.
8. Sprinkle with the remaining shredded cheese.
9. Place into the oven and bake for 15-20 minutes or until the eggs are set.
10. Garnish with reserved green onion and bacon crumbles.

Nutritional Value

Serving: 1serving | Calories: 271kcal | Carbohydrates: 11g | Protein: 17g | Fat: 17g

5. Breakfast Skillet: Two Ways

Prep Time: 10 Mins Cook Time: 20 Mins

Total Time: 30 Mins Servings: 2

Ingredients

- 2 Tbsp oil
- 3-4 medium red potatoes cut into 1 inch cubes
- salt and pepper
- 2 bell peppers chopped
- 1 cup chopped, cooked ham
- 4 eggs
- 1 cup shredded cheese
- 1 green onion sliced

Instructions

1. Heat oil over medium-high heat in a large skillet.
2. Add potatoes, season with salt and pepper, and cook until tender on the inside and crispy on the outside, about 6-8 minutes.
3. Add ham and peppers and cook just until peppers are crisp-tender, 3-4 minutes.
4. Push vegetables and ham to one-half of the pan. In the other half of the pan, drizzle with oil if necessary, and crack two eggs into the open space.
5. Cook, scrambling until cooked to your desired doneness.
6. Spoon scrambled eggs on top of the vegetables and ham on one side of the skillet, spreading the vegetables and ham throughout the skillet as you do so.
7. In the vegetables on the other half of the skillet, create two spaces for eggs.
8. Crack the two remaining eggs into the spaces, sprinkle with salt and pepper, and cook for 2-3 minutes, covering if desired, until the whites of the egg are firm.
9. Sprinkle with cheese and green onion and serve.

Nutrition Information

Calories: 371cal | Carbohydrates: 31g | Protein: 20g | Fat: 19g |

6. Keto Breakfast Skillets

Prep Time: 5 minutes Cook Time: 12 minutes

Total Time: 17 minutes Servings: 1

Ingredients

- 3 Eggs Scrambled
- 1 tbsp Heavy Cream
- 1 tsp Chives Optional
- ⅛ tsp Real Salt
- ⅓ cup Shredded Cheese

Instructions

1. Pre Heat Oven to 375 Degrees F.
2. Sprinkle shredded cheese in the skillet and heat on the stovetop over medium heat until cheese has fully melted and begun to form a golden crust on the edges, about 4-5 Minutes
3. Add in whatever toppings you like in your skillet
4. Whisk 3 Eggs Per serving along with heavy cream, salt, and chives, then pour into skillet and place in the oven for 10-12 minutes until fully cooked.
5. Eggs will be puffed up at first but will deflate a few minutes after removing from the oven.

Nutritional Value

Calories: 352kcal | Carbohydrates: 2g | Protein: 25g | Fat: 26g |

7. Easy Skillet Breakfast Nachos

Prep Time: 10 Mins Total Time: 35 Mins Servings: 4

Ingredients

- 4 cups Multigrain Tortilla Chips
- 4 eggs
- 1/4 cup milk
- 1/4 tsp. red pepper flakes
- 1/2 teaspoon salt
- 1 1/4 cups cheddar cheese, grated
- 1 cup black beans, drained and rinsed
- 3/4 cup cherry tomatoes, chopped
- 1/3 cup red peppers, chopped
- 1/4 cup green onions, minced
- 2 Tbsp fresh cilantro, minced
- 1 avocado, sliced or diced
- Sour cream and salsa for serving

Instructions

1. preheat oven to low broil. Place about 2 cups of chips in a cast-iron skillet or on a baking sheet, then sprinkle with 1/2 cup black beans and 1/2 cup cheese.
2. Set aside.
3. In a bowl, whisk together eggs, milk, red pepper flakes, and salt.
4. Heat a separate non-stick skillet over medium heat and add egg mixture.
5. Let eggs sit undisturbed until they start to set around the edges, about 2 minutes.
6. Using a rubber spatula, push the eggs from the edges into the center. Continue until eggs are just set. Remove the pan from the heat.
7. Put the cast iron skillet in preheated oven for 2 minutes, until cheese is just melted. Remove and sprinkle with half of the eggs, then top with an additional layer of chips.
8. Top with remaining eggs, beans, tomatoes, red peppers, and finally, cheese. Put back in the oven for another 3 minutes, until cheese is melted.
9. Garnish with green onions, cilantro, and avocado. Serve with sour cream and salsa if desired.

Nutrition Information

Calories: 510| Total Fat: 30g| Protein: 22g| Total Carbohydrate:37g| Sugars: 4g

8. Easy Breakfast Skillet

Prep Time: 10 Mins Cook Time: 25 Mins

Total Time: 35 Mins Servings: 4

Ingredients

- 1 tablespoon oil (canola or vegetable oil)
- 15 ounces diced frozen hash browns (about 2.5 cups)
- 8 slices cooked bacon, chopped
- 10-12 fully cooked sausage links, chopped
- 3-6 eggs
- 3/4 cup shredded cheddar cheese
- Salt and pepper

Instructions

1. Preheat oven to 400 degrees F. Bake at 400 for 8-10 minutes
2. Heat oil in an oven-safe skillet over medium-high heat.
3. Add frozen potatoes. Cook the potatoes, tossing them gently until they begin to get golden brown on the edges.
4. Season the potatoes with salt and pepper. Add the chopped bacon and sausage. And cook, tossing, for 2 minutes.
5. Smooth everything into an even layer in the skillet and then makes a little well where you want to crack each egg.
6. Crack the eggs into the well and sprinkle them with a little salt and pepper.
7. Sprinkle shredded cheese evenly over the top.
8. Bake for 8-12 minutes or until cheese is melted and eggs are cooked to your liking. (In my oven 10 minutes Servingsed perfect over-medium eggs.)

Nutritional Value

Calories: 478kcal| Carbohydrates: 20g| Protein: 25g| Fat: 33g|

9. Cast-Iron Delicoius Breakfast

Servings: 4 Prep Time: 24 mins Total Time: 40 mins

Ingredients

- 2 tbsp. extra virgin olive oil
- 1 ½ lb. red potatoes, coarsely chopped
- 1 red bell pepper, seeded and chopped
- ½ c. yellow onion, chopped
- 2 clove(s) garlic, minced
- ½ tsp. kosher sea salt
- ¼ tsp. black pepper
- 4 oz. fully cooked Spanish chorizo, sliced
- 1 (4-oz) can mild diced green chilies
- 1 c. shredded Cheddar cheese (4 oz)
- 4 large pasteurized eggs
- Fresh cilantro, for garnish

Instructions

1. Preheat oven to 400°F.
2. Heat olive oil over medium heat in a 10-in. cast-iron skillet.
3. Add potatoes, bell pepper, onion, garlic, salt, and black pepper.
4. Cook for 12 to 15 minutes or until potatoes is tender and golden brown, stirring occasionally.

5. Add chorizo and chiles; stir until combined. Sprinkle cheese evenly over the potato mixture.

6. Create four 2-in. indentations in the potato-chorizo mixture, using the back of a spoon.

7. Crack one egg into each indentation, ensuring the egg is in contact with the bottom of the skillet.

8. Bake for 12 to 15 minutes or until egg whites are set and yolks begin to thicken.

9. If desired, garnish with cilantro.

Nutrition Facts

Calories: 313kcal | Fat: 34g | Carbohydrates: 20g: | Protein: 24g.

10. Hearty Breakfast Skillet

Prep Time: 5 minutes Cook Time: 20 minutes

Servings:2

Ingredients

- ¼ Cup olive oil
- 5 cups frozen shredded hash browns
- 1 teaspoon chili powder
- 1 teaspoon garlic powder
- 1 Tbsp cumin
- ¼ tsp. fennel seeds
- ½ teaspoon kosher salt
- 2 green onions, thinly sliced
- ¼ cup shredded cheddar cheese, plus a sprinkle more
- 1 Tbsp butter
- 4 eggs

For The Garnish:
Salsa, fresh cilantro (optional)

Instructions

1. Cook The Hash Browns: Heat the olive oil in a large oven-proof or cast iron skillet and add the hash browns, flipping occasionally until browned. At 6 minutes, add the chili powder, garlic powder, cumin, fennel seeds, and kosher salt. Cook another for about 6 minutes until browned, continuing to flip so they don't stick.

2. Add The Cheese And Eggs: Reduce the heat to low. Add the green onions (reserving a handful for the garnish) and cheese and mix it in. Make divots for the eggs (down to the bare pan) and add ¼ Tbsp butter into each well. Crack 1 egg into each well, and top each with a pinch of kosher salt. Add a sprinkle of additional shredded cheese on top.

3. Cook The Eggs On The Stovetop: Increase the heat to medium-low and cook for 3 minutes on the stove. Meanwhile, preheat the broiler.

4. Finish In The Broiler: Transfer the skillet to the broiler and cook for 3 to 4 minutes until the whites of the eggs are set.

5. Serve: Garnish with salsa, the reserved green onions, and fresh cilantro. Serve warm.

Nutritional Value

Calories: 216 kcal Total Fat 25.1g | Carbohydrate 20.4g | Protein 10.5g

11. Tasty Breakfast

Total Time: 30 Minutes Servings: 4

Ingredients

- 1–1 1/2 pounds frozen hash browns, either shredded or diced
- 4 eggs
- 7–8 slices bacon, fully cooked and chopped into 1/2 inch bits
- 1 green pepper, thinly sliced in half circles or diced
- 1/2 medium yellow onion, thinly sliced in half circles or diced
- 1/2 cup shredded cheddar cheese
- 1–2 Tbsp olive oil
- 1 teaspoon garlic powder
- 1 tsp. onion powder
- 1/2 teaspoon paprika
- 1–2 Tbsp fresh chopped parsley
- Salt and pepper, to taste

Direction

1. Preheat oven to 400° F. If baking bacon, you can add it now for about 15-20 minutes.

2. Bring 1 tablespoon of oil to medium heat in an oven-safe cast-iron skillet.

3. Add peppers and onions and cook, tossing occasionally, until golden and tender, about 5 minutes.

4. Add potatoes and all spices. Cook potatoes, tossing occasionally, until golden and starting to crisp about 5-7 minutes. You may need to add a Tbsp of oil to golden up.
5. Evenly arrange potatoes in the skillet and top with cheese and chopped bacon.
6. Create 4 small impressions in the potatoes and carefully crack 4 eggs around the edges of the skillet, ensuring the yolks stay intact.
7. Sometimes it helps to crack the eggs in a small prep bowl and carefully slide them into the skillet.
8. Bake for 10 minutes or until egg whites is no longer clear. You want the egg yolks still runny! Sprinkle with fresh parsley and serve.
9. For this recipe, I used a bag of frozen shredded hash brown potatoes.
10. You can always use homemade shredded potatoes, it's just a little more work upfront. If you can't find shredded potatoes, diced frozen potatoes work just as well.
11. You can easily add breakfast sausage as well by cooking first in the skillet (before pepper and onions) and chopping/dicing. Top before baking along with the bacon.

Nutritional Value

Calories: 352| Fat: 31.9g| Carbohydrates: 26.5g| Protein: 24.5g|

12. Cheesy Bacon And Egg Hash

Prep Time: 10 Mins Cook Time: 25 Mins

Total Time: 35 Mins Servings: 4

Ingredients

- 24 oz (700 g) potatoes, (about 4 medium-sized), scrubbed clean and peeled
- 2 Tbsp olive oil, (or coconut oil)
- 7 oz (200 g) diced bacon, (trimmed of fat)
- 2 scallions or spring onions, (shallots) trimmed and finely sliced
- 4 large eggs
- 1/4 cup shredded mozzarella cheese (or cheddar)
- Cracked pepper to season

Instructions

1. Dice potatoes into small 3/4-inch cubes.
2. Heat the oil in a large cast-iron skillet or pan over medium heat. Fry the potatoes in the hot oil and cook while stirring occasionally, until golden and crispy (about 20 minutes). To speed up cooking time, cover the pan with a lid, checking the potatoes every 4-5 minutes or so to stir them (this takes about 15 minutes).
3. Add the bacon pieces to the pan and fry while stirring occasionally for 10 minutes until crisp. The potatoes will be golden with crisp edges, while soft on the inside. Add the spring onions; stir them through and season with pepper (optional).
4. Using a wooden spoon or spatula, make four wells in the hash, crack an egg into each well and arrange the mozzarella around each egg. Fry until the whites are set and the eggs are cooked to your liking.
5. Serve immediately.

Nutritional Value

Calories: 413kcal | Carbohydrates: 18g | Protein: 17g | Fat: 28g

13. Cheesy Skillet Breakfast

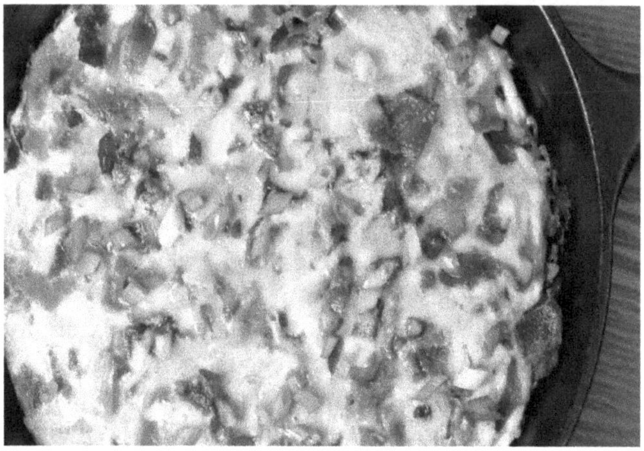

Prep Time: 15 mins Cook Time: 30 mins

Servings: 4

Ingredients

- 4 cups potatoes washed and cut into cubes
- ½ cup red onions diced
- ½ cup sweet peppers diced
- ½ cup grape tomatoes or diced tomatoes

- 4 ounces bacon cooked and diced
- 4 ounces sausage crumbled
- 4 ounces Cheddar shredded
- 8 large eggs
- 1 tbsp parsley fine chop for garnish
- Sea Salt to taste
- Black Pepper to taste

Instructions

1. Preheat oven to 450 degrees Fahrenheit
2. prep all ingredients
3. mix diced potatoes with enough olive oil to lightly coat them then season heavily with black pepper and sea salt. Place the potatoes on a parchment-lined baking sheet and place them into a preheated oven for 20 minutes.
4. In a Cast Iron or regular frying pan, cook diced bacon and loose chorizo. Chorizo will finish cooking first (about 5 minutes) remove it from the pan and allow excess grease to drain.
5. Continue cooking bacon until semi crisp (3-5 additional minutes). Remove from pan, allowing grease to drain. Remove the remainder of the grease, leaving a tablespoon to sautee the onions and peppers.
6. Set sausage and bacon aside till needed.
7. Place the onions and peppers into the heated pan with 1 Tbsp of the grease pulled from the pan. Cook for about 2 minutes.
8. When the potatoes are done, remove the baking sheet from the oven. Spread the cooked sausage, bacon, onions, and peppers onto the potatoes and gently mix.
9. Add shredded Cabot Cheese to the top of the mixture and sprinkle with chopped parsley.
10. Place baking sheet back into the oven for 2-3 minutes until the cheese has slightly melted.
11. Remove pan from oven and set the oven to broil.
12. Carefully take parchment paper by both ends and pour the ingredients into the cast iron skillet (you can use a casserole dish instead).
13. Once in the pan, make little wells in the mixture for the eggs. Gently place a whole egg in each well.
14. Season the eggs with sea salt and black pepper. Sprinkle chopped parsley over the top of the ingredients for color.
15. Place Cast Iron pan under the broiler and allow eggs to cook (about 3-5 minutes). Once the whites have solidified the eggs are done. I like my eggs loose and sunny side up, so I cook them just long enough. Feel free to cook them longer.
16. You can also use the alternate method of covering the pan and cooking on the stovetop allowing the steam to cook the eggs. Or fry the eggs separately and place them on top of the individual servings of the potato mixture.
17. Remove from oven and serve immediately. I served mine with flour tortillas.

Nutritional Value

Calories: 584kcal | Carbohydrates: 25g | Protein: 34g | Fat: 38g | Saturated Fat: 16g

14. Sausage and Bacon with Onion and Mushroom

Prep Time: 10 mins Cook Time: 30 mins

Total Time: 40 mins Serving: 4

Ingredients

- 1 tsp oil
- 2 sausages
- 3 streaky bacon rashers
- 1/2 onion
- 50 g baby mushrooms cleaned and halved
- 50 g cherry tomatoes
- 1 egg

Instructions

1. Heat the pan over medium-high heat.
2. Add the oil, then the sausages and onions. Let cook for 4 or 5 minutes, turning the sausages occasionally to color each side.
3. Add in the mushrooms and let sit on the cut side for a few minutes to turn golden.
4. Next add in the bacon, followed by the cherry tomatoes, and finally crack the egg in the center of the pan.
5. Enjoy the process of cooking this breakfast. Try not to rush it, just kick back and relax.

Nutrition Facts

Calories: 216 | Fat: 76g | Carbohydrates: 10g | Protein: 37g

15. Potatoes Breakfast

Prep Time: 15 Mins Cook Time: 30 Mins

Total Time: 45 Mins Servings: 4

Ingredients

- 3 Tbsp butter
- 4 red potatoes chopped
- 2 tsp vegetable oil
- 1 1/2 tsp seasoned salt divided
- 1/2 tsp salt
- 1/2 tsp ground black pepper divided
- 8 oz bacon 1/2" diced pieces
- 2 garlic cloves minced
- 4 eggs
- 1/2 c. extra-sharp cheddar cheese

Instructions

1. Preheat grill to 400 degrees.
2. In a bowl mix together diced potatoes, vegetable oil, seasoned salt, salt, and ground black pepper.
3. Place cast-iron skillet on the grill. Heat butter in skillet. Add potato mixture and bacon to skillet; close the grill lid and cook until brown and tender; stirring occasionally. Add garlic right before potatoes are done cooking and saute for about 1 minute.
4. With the back of a spoon, make four wells in the potato mixture; break eggs into wells. Close the grill lid and bake until egg whites are completely set and yolks begin to thicken but are not hard. This will take about 9-11 minutes.
5. Open grill and sprinkle cheese on the skillet. Close the grill lid and let the cheese melt for a few minutes.

Nutritional Value

Calories: 664kcal | Carbohydrates: 35g | Protein: 24g | Fat: 47g |

16. Bacon, Egg & Crispy Potato Breakfast Skillet

Servings : 8 Prep Time: 10 Minutes Cook Time: 20 Minutes Total Time: 30 Minutes

Ingredients

- 2 pounds tiny baby potatoes (the tiniest you can find)
- 1-2 cups reduced-sodium chicken stock or broth
- 4 T unsalted butter
- 6 large eggs (beaten well with 1 T water)
- 1 cup shredded cheddar cheese
- 8 slices thick-cut bacon (cooked and crumbled)
- 1/2 cup sour cream
- 1/2 red bell pepper (diced)
- 1 jalapeno (minced)
- 2 green onions (chopped)
- 1/4 cup chopped flat-leaf parsley

Instructions

1. Place one layer of baby potatoes in a 12-inch cast-iron skillet, fitting slightly snugly. Pour chicken stock over potatoes just until halfway up their sides. Bring to a boil over medium-high heat. Reduce heat to medium, cover skillet, and cook for 5 minutes.
2. Remove the cover from the skillet and cook another 5 minutes. Cut butter into four pieces and lay each piece of butter in a different spot over the potatoes, allowing it to melt. DO NOT STIR. Keep cooking until all liquid has evaporated and you hear a sizzling sound – that sound means that the potatoes are now starting to brown.
3. Using something flat-bottomed (I use a tamper but anything flat-bottomed will do), gently press down on each potato to flatten (it's okay if they split). Now just

leave them alone to brown – no stirring – for another 5 minutes, checking the bottoms occasionally.

4. Once the bottoms of the potatoes have browned, pour beaten eggs over potatoes. Reduce heat to medium-low, cover, and cook until the egg on the side is starting to look done (about 3 minutes). Place skillet under broiler and, watching carefully, cook the top of the eggs until just done.

5. Remove the skillet from the oven. Top cooked eggs with cheese, then bacon, sour cream, and remaining ingredients. Serve immediately.

Nutrition Information

Calories: 534kcal Total Fat: 22g | Carbohydrates: 28g | | Protein: 17g

17. Cowboy Skillet Breakfast (Alternative Version)

Prep Time: 5 Mins Cook Time: 20 Mins

Total Time: 25 Mins

Ingredients

- 1/4 pound bulk hot pork sausage
- 1/2 red bell pepper chopped
- 1/4 small onion chopped
- 1 medium-sized red potato cubed into 1/4 – 1/2 inch pieces
- 1/4 cup shredded cheddar cheese
- 2 eggs Note: Use 1 egg per person for sunny side up and 2 eggs per person if scrambling eggs
- 2 Tbsp butter
- 2 green onions chopped
- Salt and pepper to taste

Instructions

1. Get a campfire going to create campfire coals for cooking over medium heat. If you are using a propane camp stove, set it up for cooking on a level surface.

2. Heat the cast-iron skillet over the heat. Camp Cooking Tip: Use a 10-inch cast-iron skillet if cooking for one or two people and a 12-inch skillet if you are feeding 3-6 campers.

3. Once the skillet is preheated, add the sausage to brown it, breaking it up into crumbles as it cooks.

4. Now, add the butter, bell pepper, onion, potatoes, salt, and pepper, stirring occasionally, and cook covered until the potatoes are softened about 8 minutes. Camp Cooking Tip: If your cast iron skillet does not have a lid, you can use a lid from a cast-iron Dutch oven or aluminum foil.

5. Flatten the ingredients across the bottom of the skillet, then use a spoon to create "wells" for cooking the eggs. Be sure to leave a layer of the sausage and potato mixture at the bottom of the wells so the eggs are sitting on the food rather than directly on the bottom of the skillet pan when they cook.

6. Crack the eggs and add them into the skillet by dropping them into the wells. You can drop whole eggs for sunny side up style eggs or beaten eggs if you prefer scrambled eggs.

7. Cover and cook until the eggs are done to your desired likeness, about 3-5 minutes.

8. Sprinkle with cheese, replace the cover on the pan and let the cheese melt slightly for a few more seconds.

9. Remove the skillet from the heat and top with green onions, serve hot.

Nutritional Value

Calories: 364kcal Carbohydrates: 22g | Fat: 37g |

18. Skillet Baked Eggs With Potatoes And Bacon

Prep Time: 5 mins Cook Time: 30 mins

Total Time: 35 mins Servings: 4

Ingredients

- 1 tbsp butter
- 1 tbsp olive oil
- 4 cups medium golden Yukon potatoes, cubed
- 1 cup diced white or yellow onion
- 1 tsp granulated garlic
- 4 eggs
- 1/4 cup crumbled or chopped bacon
- Salt and pepper to taste
- 1/4 cup cheddar cheese (optional for garnish)
- 2 tbsp fresh chopped chives (optional for garnish)

Instructions

1. Preheat oven to 350 degrees.

2. On the stovetop: Heat oven-safe skillet to medium-high heat, and add butter and olive oil.
3. Once sizzling, add potatoes, and onion to the pan. Add salt, pepper to taste along with granulated garlic. Stir for 10-15 minutes, or until potatoes and onion have nice brown toasty edges.
4. Add bacon to skillet and stir. Make small well were for eggs, and gently crack and drop eggs into well, leaving the yolk intact.
5. Place skillet in the oven for 10-12 minutes, or until eggs are cooked to your desire.
6. Top with cheese and chives if desired. Serve and enjoy.

Nutrition Facts

Calories: 514kcal | Fat 28g | Carbohydrates 41g | Protein

19. Southwest Breakfast Casserole

Total Time: 40-60 minutes Serving: 4

Ingredients

- 1 bag frozen hash brown potatoes
- 4 eggs, room temp
- 1/4 cup caramelized garlic
- Salt and pepper, to taste
- 1 lb bacon
- Red bell pepper, diced
- Green bell pepper, diced
- 2 jalapeños diced and seeds removed
- 1 cup shredded cheese or more if you like
- Cooking spray

Instructions

1. Spray your cast iron skillet with cooking spray, heating it to medium to high temp.
2. Add the bacon, garlic, peppers, and fry until crisp, remove the mix, and place to the side.
3. While the bacon is cooling, pour off some of the bacon greases leaving enough to fry the hash brown potatoes on medium to high heat.
4. Once almost cooked add your bacon pepper mix and fold to combine.
5. Make four pockets and crack one egg into each one.
6. Top with the shredded cheese allowing the eggs to cook completely and the cheese to slightly melt.
7. Cover to thoroughly cook the egg to the desired doneness.
8. If desired add the diced jalapeno pepper on top for garnish.
9. Serve with salsa and or sour cream as desired.

Nutrition Information

Calories: 364kcal Total Fat: 56g | Carbohydrates: 12g | Protein: 52g

20. Tasty Breakfast Skillet With Bacon, Egg, Potato, And Cheese

Servings: 4 Prep Time: 5 minutes

Cook Time: 25 minutes

Ingredients

- 4 strips of bacon (cut into 1 inch long pieces)
- 6 cups of frozen cubed hash browns (or the same amount cubed fresh potato)
- 1/2 cup of white onion, chopped
- 1/2 tsp of salt
- 1/4 tsp of pepper
- 1/4 cup of water
- 4 large eggs
- 1 cup of Cheddar cheese, shredded
- Optional ingredients
- 2 tbs green onions, sliced
- 1 clove garlic, minced or finely chopped

Instructions

1. Place your cast iron skillet on the stovetop, at medium-high heat.
2. Cook the strips of bacon until they are good and crispy, and then remove them from the skillet. Place them to one side on some paper towels to drain off the excess fat.
3. Keep around 2 tbs of the bacon fat in the skillet (this will add flavor to your breakfast skillet).
4. Add your pre-cubed frozen hash brown to the pan along with the sliced white onion. If you're using raw potato instead, you should cube it or shred it before adding it (depending on your preferred breakfast hash recipe). Fry the onions and potatoes in the bacon

drippings for 2-3 min, and then add the water and place a lid on the skillet.

5. Cook for another 15 min, removing the cover and flipping the potatoes a couple of times during the process (to ensure they end up crispy on all sides).

6. If you're using garlic, add it and stir it through the mixture. Cook for another minute. If not, skip straight to adding salt and pepper to taste.

7. Use a wooden spoon to create 4 round wells in the potato mixture (the surface of the skillet should be exposed in those areas).

8. Drizzle a small amount of oil into the well, no more than the size of a quarter (or a 1/4 tsp of butter). Crack one of your eggs into each of the wells, and replace the lid.

9. Move the skillet to low heat and leave the eggs to cook. For firm whites with a runny yolk, you'll need around 8-9 min. Add 1-2 min more for medium, and 3-4 min more if you prefer your egg yolks hard.

10. Around 2 min before the eggs are cooked to your liking, sprinkle the shredded cheese and chopped bacon over the top (you can crumble the bacon into bacon bits if you prefer), and top with finely chopped green onions if you've decided to include them.

11. Allow eggs to finish cooking.

12. Divide into portions and serve up a delicious skillet breakfast!

Nutritional Facts

Calories: 455kcal Carbohydrates: 20g| Protein: 25g| Fat: 33g

21. Mountain Breakfast Skillet

Prep Time: 5 minutes Cook Time: 20 minutes

Total Time: 25 minutes Servings: 2

Ingredients

- 4 Tbsp avocado or olive oil
- 4 cups frozen shredded hashbrowns
- 1 tsp. sea salt, divided
- ½ large onion (or 1 ¼ cup), cut into a ¼" dice
- 1 red pepper, seeded & cut into a ¼" dice
- 1 large or 2 small (or 2 ¼ cups) zucchini, cut into quarters vertically, then sliced width-wise into ⅛" coins
- 12 oz. cooked apple chicken sausage, cut into ½" cubes
- 6 large eggs
- ¼ tsp. freshly cracked black pepper
- ¾ cup shredded light Mexican cheese blend (or cheddar cheese)

Instructions

1. Preheat oven to 375 degrees Fahrenheit. Heat 2 Tbsp oil in a 12 inch cast iron skillet, (or other oven-safe & non-stick skillet) over medium heat.

2. Add the hashbrowns and ½ teaspoon salt to the skillet and cook for 6-7 minutes, flipping just once or twice through cooking, or until the hash browns are cooked through and starting to turn golden. Remove the hashbrowns from the pan.

3. Add the remaining 2 Tbsp of oil to the skillet. Add the onion, pepper, and zucchini and saute for 4-5 minutes, stirring frequently, or until the onions are fragrant and are just starting to turn translucent.

4. Add the chicken sausage and remaining ½ teaspoon salt to the veggies and cook, continuing to stir frequently, or until the sausage is heated through and the zucchini is a bright green color.

5. Stir the hash browns back into the veggie mixture. Turn off the stovetop heat.

6. Make 6 wells in the potato mixture. Crack one egg into each well. Sprinkle the eggs with cracked pepper and shredded cheese.

7. Add the skillet to the oven and bake for 10-15 minutes, or until the eggs are cooked through to your desired level of doneness (10 minutes should leave the eggs still running inside; 15 should have them more firm).

8. Remove the skillet from the oven and serve hot!

Nutrition Information

Calories: 474kcal Total Fat: 24g | Carbohydrates: 29g | Protein: 27g

22. Bacon, Egg, And Potato Breakfast Skillet

Servings: 4 Prep Time: 5 Minutes Cook Time: 25 Minutes Total Time: 30 Minutes

Ingredients

- 4 strips bacon cut into 1-inch pieces
- 6 cups (about 3/4 of 30-ounce bag) frozen cubed southern style hash browns, fresh potatoes can also be used
- 1/2 cup white onion
- 1/2 tsp. salt
- 1/4 teaspoon pepper
- 1/4 cup water
- 1 clove minced garlic, (this is optional)
- 4 large eggs
- 1 cup shredded cheddar cheese
- 2 Tbsp sliced green onions, (optional)

Instructions

1. In a large skillet, cook bacon over medium-high heat until crisp. Remove bacon and drain on paper towels, leaving about 2 Tbsp of drippings in the skillet.
2. Add onion and potatoes to the pan stirring to coat in bacon drippings and cook for a couple of minutes. Add water and cover the skillet. Cook for 15 minutes or until soft, only flipping once or twice. When you let the potatoes sit without flipping, they get nice and brown. Stir in garlic, and cook for a minute. Add more salt and pepper to taste.
3. Make four wells in the potatoes, exposing the skillet underneath. Carefully, crack the egg in each spot. Cover skillet and let eggs cook over low heat until egg whites are set about 8-10 minutes. Sprinkle cheese and bacon on top during the last couple of minutes of cooking. Sprinkle with green onions and serve.

Nutrition Information

Calories: 496kcal | Fat 29g | Carbohydrates 48g | Protein 8g

23. Loaded Veggie Breakfast Skillet

Prep Time: 10 minutes Cook Time: 40 minutes

Total Time: 50 minutes Servings: 4

Ingredients

- 450 g potatoes, scrubbed, skin on, and cut into 2cm cubes I used Maris Piper, but any potato will do.
- 3 tbsp olive oil, divided
- ½ tsp sea salt, divided
- ½ tsp cracked black pepper, divided
- 1 small onion, (100g) cut in half then thinly sliced
- 1 medium green bell pepper (110g) pith and seeds removed then thinly sliced
- 1 medium red bell pepper (110g) pith and seeds removed then thinly sliced
- 230 g portobello mushroom (3 large mushrooms) wiped clean then sliced
- 1 tsp dried oregano
- 2 cloves of garlic minced
- A scant ¼ tsp dried red chili flakes optional
- 90 g spinach
- 4 large eggs
- 2 tbsp freshly squeezed lemon juice

For Serving

- A small handful of fresh flat-leaf parsley chopped
- 2 spring onions chopped
- Lemon wedges
- Dried red chili flakes

Instructions

1. Preheat the oven to 200 degrees C, 392F. I use an electric fan-assisted oven, please adjust according to your oven.
2. Place the potatoes on a baking tray, pour over 2 Tbsp of oil add ¼ teaspoon each of salt and black pepper. Toss well then bake in the oven for 30 minutes turning the potatoes halfway through cooking.
3. While the potatoes are roasting, cook up the veggies.
4. Heat the remaining oil in a skillet, add the onion and cook over medium heat until soft, about 10 minutes.
5. Add the peppers and cook for 5 minutes. Once the peppers are a little soft add the mushrooms, garlic, oregano, salt, pepper, and chili flakes. Cook for another 5 minutes.
6. Now adds the spinach, I add half first, let that wilt down then add the remaining spinach. Add the lemon juice and stir well.
7. Once the potatoes are cooked transfer them to the skillet and give everything a good stir. Check the seasoning now and add more if necessary.
8. Make 4 little wells in the skillet, break one egg into each well. Place a lid over the skillet, this will help cook

your eggs quicker. Once the eggs are cooked to your taste turn off the heat.

9. Sprinkle over the parsley and chopped spring onion and serve.

10. Serve with lemon wedges and more red chili flakes if you like.

Nutritional Value

Calories: 289kcal| Carbohydrates: 27g| Protein: 11.4g| Fat: 15.9g

24. Country Breakfast Skillet

Prep Time: 20 mins Cook Time: 25 mins

Total Time: 45 mins Servings: 4 to 6 servings

Ingredients

- 6 slices bacon (cut into 2-inch pieces)
- 1/4 cup chopped green bell pepper
- 2 Tbsp finely chopped onion
- 6 cups cubed cooked potatoes
- 1/2 cup shredded sharp cheddar cheese
- 6 large eggs, lightly beaten
- Salt, to taste
- Ground pepper, to taste

Instructions

1. Gather the ingredients.

2. In a large, heavy skillet, cook the bacon over moderate heat until crisp.

3. Remove the bacon to drain on paper towels.

4. Crumble the bacon and set it aside.

5. Pour off all but 3 Tbsp of bacon drippings from the skillet. Heat these 3 Tbsp of drippings in the pan over medium-high heat until sizzling.

6. Add the bell pepper, onion, and potatoes. Cook, stirring gently until the potato cubes are browned.

7. Sprinkle the shredded cheese over the mixture and stir until melted.

8. Add the beaten eggs and cook, stirring gently, until the eggs are set.

9. Season with salt and pepper. Sprinkle the crumbled bacon over the eggs. Serve immediately.

Nutrition Facts

Calories: 296kcal Total Fat: 15g Total Carbohydrate: 37g| g| Protein: 19g|

25. Mountain Man Breakfast

Total Time: 1 hour 30 mins Servings 8

Ingredients

- 10 small red potatoes or (2 pounds frozen hash browns)
- 1 lb bacon cut into bite-sized pieces
- 1 lb ground breakfast pork sausage
- 1 white onion chopped
- 1 red bell pepper diced
- 1 roasted poblano pepper diced
- Kent's Original Seasoning to taste or salt and pepper
- 1 cup shredded pepper jack cheese
- 1 cup shredded cheddar cheese
- 10 eggs divided

Instructions

1. Heat the oven to 350 degrees F. Lightly butter a 12-inch Dutch oven.

2. If using red potatoes, grate the potatoes into a bowl and cover them with water. Set aside. Skip to the next step if using hash browns.

3. Add the bacon to the Dutch oven over medium-high heat. Cook until browned, about 6 minutes, stirring occasionally. Leave a little bacon grease, but drain any excess and remove the bacon to drain on a paper towel.

4. Return to the Dutch oven or skillet and crumble in the sausage and cook until it begins to brown about 6 minutes, stirring occasionally. Stir in the onion, bell pepper, and poblano.

5. Drain the potatoes from the water and pat dry with a towel. Stir into the sausage mixture and cook until the peppers and onions are tender. Season to taste with Kent's Original Seasoning.

6. Place 6 of the eggs in a medium bowl and whisk until smooth. Pour the eggs evenly over the sausage mixture. Sprinkle the bacon on top. Bake for about 45 minutes or until the eggs set up.

7. Sprinkle the cheeses evenly over the top and cook for another 5 minutes or until the cheese melts. Crack the remaining eggs on top and bake until the eggs are sunny side up, about 5 minutes. Serve warm.

Nutritional Value

Calories: 256kcal Carbohydrates: 11g | Protein: 17g | Fat: 17g |

POULTRY RECIPES

26. Chicken Breasts With Potatoes And Leeks

Servings: 4 Prep Time: 10 mins Cook Time: 45 mins

Ingredients

- 4 bone-in Chicken Breasts
- 2 tbsp olive oil
- 2 leeks, sliced and rinsed
- 1 lb baby Yukon gold potatoes, cut in half
- 1 cup chicken stock
- 2 tbsp butter
- 1 tbsp Italian Seasoning
- 1 tsp chopped fresh thyme
- 3 garlic cloves, minced

Instructions

1. Preheat oven to 425 degrees.
2. Season the chicken breasts, liberally, with salt and pepper. Set aside.
3. Heat the olive oil in the skillet over medium-high heat until shimmering.
4. Add the chicken breasts to the skillet, skin side down. Cook until golden brown and crispy, approximately 5-7 minutes.
5. Flip the chicken over and cook for an additional 5 minutes.
6. Transfer the chicken to a platter and keep warm.
7. Add the leeks and potatoes to the skillet. Cook until the leeks have softened, stirring occasionally, approximately 5 minutes.
8. Stir in the chicken stock, butter, garlic, and herbs. Bring the mixture to a boil and return the chicken to the pan, skin side up.
9. Transfer the skillet to the oven and bake for 20-25 or until an instant-read thermometer registers 165 degrees.
10. Remove the skillet from the oven and allow the chicken to rest for 5 minutes.
11. Serve the chicken with the potatoes and leeks. Spoon the pan sauce over the chicken, if desired.

Nutritional Value

Calories: 516kcal| Carbohydrates: 30g| Protein: 42g| Fat: 25g|

27. Cast-Iron Chicken Breast

Prep Time: 10 minutes Cook Time: 25 minutes

Total Time: 35 minutes Servings: 2

Ingredients

- 2 chicken breast about 200 g/ 7 oz each
- 1 organic lemon
- A small handful of parsley
- 1 teaspoon honey
- 2 Tbsp olive oil divided
- Fine sea salt and pepper

Instructions

1. Wash and zest the lemon. Juice it, but start only with half the juice when making the marinade.
2. Make The Marinade: Mix the lemon zest, lemon juice, parsley leaves, honey, and 1 Tbsp olive oil in a small blender. Process until you have a smooth paste. Add salt and pepper to taste and more lemon juice or honey according to your liking.
3. Marinate Chicken: Place the chicken in a shallow dish and pour the marinade over. Turn the chicken a few times in the container to coat all over. Cover with plastic

foil and leave to marinate in the fridge for a few hours or overnight.

4. If you marinate it for a shorter time, like 30 minutes, leave it on the counter, if not take it out of the fridge at least 30 minutes before cooking to make sure that the meat reaches room temperature.

5. Cook: Heat a cast-iron skillet very well. Heat the remaining oil, add the chicken, turn the heat to medium-low and cook for a total of 20 to 25 minutes, turning several times in between but not disturbing the chicken for the first 6-7 minutes or so.

6. After the initial 6-7 minutes, if you notice that the chicken breast gets too dark too soon, lower the heat and move the chicken around in the skillet.

7. Check if the chicken breasts are cooked through by inserting a skewer in the thickest part of the chicken breast, the juices should run clear.

8. You could start checking shortly before the first 20 minutes have ended to ensure that you don't overcook the chicken, especially if the chicken pieces weigh a bit less than 200 g/ 7 oz.

9. Smaller chicken breast pieces weighing about 120-150 g/ 4.2 – 5.3 oz should be ready in 18 to 20 minutes.

10. Or use a meat thermometer; the internal temperature should be between 73 – 82 degrees Celsius/165 – 180 degrees Fahrenheit.

11. Serve immediately with side dishes of your choice (most anything fits) or let cool and serve on a salad.

Nutritional Value

Calories: 341kcal | Carbohydrates: 7g | Protein: 38g | Fat: 18g

28. Cast Iron Pan-Roasted Chicken Breasts

Prep Time: 5 minutes Cook Time: 30 minutes

Total Time: 35 minutes

Ingredients

- 2 bone-in chicken breasts
- Salt and pepper
- 1 Tbsp butter
- 1 Tbsp oil

Instructions

1. Preheat oven to 425 degrees.

2. Preheat your cast iron pan on top of the stove for just a few minutes.

3. Generously salt and pepper the skin side of the chicken breasts.

4. Add the butter and oil at the same time.

5. Once the butter and oil are melted and heated, add the chicken breasts skin side down.

6. Allow them to sear for a few minutes.

7. Salt and pepper on the other side of the chicken breasts.

8. Flip the chicken breasts and allow the other side to sear for another minute or two.

9. Place the cast iron pan in the preheated oven and continue to cook the chicken for about 20 to 30 minutes or until the chicken reaches an internal temperature of 165 degrees.

10. Allow the chicken to rest for 5 minutes before slicing.

Nutritional Value

Calories: 374 kcal Total Fat: 17g | Protein: 37g

29. Chicken And Bell Peppers Skillet

Servings: 4 People Prep Time: 10 Minutes

Cook Time: 25 Minutes Total Time: 35 Minutes

Ingredients

For The Chicken

- 4 free-range organic chicken thighs - bone-in and skin-on
- 1 teaspoon paprika
- 1 teaspoon garlic powder
- ½ tsp. Italian seasoning
- Salt and black pepper
- 1 tablespoon olive oil

For The Bell Peppers

- 2 large bell peppers - 1 red and 1 orange, sliced
- 1 small red onion - sliced
- 1 tsp. garlic clove - minced
- ½ teaspoon paprika
- 1/8 teaspoon red chili flakes or ground chili pepper

- Salt and black pepper

Instructions

1. Heat a cast-iron skillet over medium-high heat on the stove. Meanwhile, in a large bowl place chicken and all the seasonings for the chicken. Mix everything well to combine.
2. Overhead view of a large glass bowl containing chicken thighs
3. Add olive oil to the skillet. Add chicken in skillet, skin side down, and cook 4-6 minutes or until browned. Turn chicken over and cook for 1 minute. Set aside (chicken won't be cooked yet).
4. close up of cast iron skillet containing chicken thighs
5. Remove skillet from the heat and add peppers, onion, garlic, paprika, red chili flakes, and salt and peppers. Stir everything well to combine.
6. overhead view of a cast iron containing slices of bell pepper and onions
7. Arrange chicken on top of the peppers and onions and place the skillet in the pre-heat over. Bake at 400°F for 15-20 minutes or until the chicken gets an internal temperature of 165°F. Enjoy!

Nutritional Value

Calories: 291kcal Carbohydrates: 9g| Protein: 18g| Fat: 18g|

30. Cast Iron Chicken Breast and Potatoes

Prep Time: 15 minutes Cook Time: 1 hour

Total Time: 1 hour 15 minutes Servings: 4

Ingredients

For The Chicken:

- 1 1/2-2 lbs chicken cut up
- 1/2 tsp cumin
- 1/2 tsp Cajun seasoning
- 1/2 tsp salt
- 2 grated garlic cloves
- 2 tbsp olive oil + extra for frying

For The Vegetables:

- 1 1/2 lbs baby potatoes
- 1/2 lb. baby carrots
- 8 oz crimini mushrooms
- 1/2 medium onion
- 1/4 tsp cumin
- 1/2 tsp Cajun seasoning
- 1 tsp salt
- 1 grated garlic clove
- 4 tbsp olive oil

Instructions

1. In a bowl combine the chicken, cumin, Cajun seasoning, salt, 2 grated garlic cloves, and olive oil.
2. Heat a cast-iron pan over high heat and brown both sides of each chicken piece.
3. Meanwhile cut the potatoes in half. Then cut mushrooms and onions into wedges.
4. In a separate bowl, combine the potatoes, baby carrots, mushrooms, onion, cumin, Cajun seasoning, salt, 1 grated garlic clove, and olive oil.
5. Place into the cast iron pan and cover with foil. Bake at 400 degrees Fahrenheit for 1 hour. Remove the foil in the last 15 minutes of cooking.

Nutritional Value

Calories: 689kcal | Carbohydrates: 36.8g | Protein: 70.8g | Fat: 28.2g |

31. Easy Pan Seared Chicken Breast

Prep Time: 7 minutes Cook Time: 8 minutes

Total Time: 50 minute Servings: 4

Ingredients

- 2 boneless skinless chicken breasts
- 1/2 tsp salt
- 1/4 tsp black pepper
- 1/2 tsp garlic powder
- 1 tbsp avocado oil

Instructions

1. Slice chicken breasts in half horizontally so you have 2 thinner pieces from each chicken breast
2. Mix salt, pepper, and garlic powder (or any seasonings you are using) in a small mixing bowl
3. Season all 4 chicken breast pieces on top and bottom with the seasoning mixture
4. Heat oil in a large cast-iron skillet over medium heat

5. Once the oil is hot, add the seasoned chicken breast to the pan – if you only have a small cast-iron skillet, cook the chicken in batches

6. Cook the chicken over medium heat for 8 minutes, flipping every 2 minutes, the flipping is crucial for getting an evenly cooked piece of chicken!!

7. After 8 minutes the chicken should be fully cooked through with an internal temp of 165F. If it is not, continue cooking for an additional 2 minutes

8. Remove the chicken from the pan immediately and allow to rest on a cutting board for at least 5 minutes before slicing to lock in moisture

9. Enjoy immediately or store in an airtight container in the fridge for up to 4 days.

Nutrition Facts

Calories: 341kcal Total Fat: 13g| Total Carbohydrate: 0.7g | Protein: 51.2g

32. Salt And Pepper Roast Chicken

Prep Time: 15 minutes Cook Time: 45 minutes

Total Time: 1 hour Servings: 4

Ingredients

- 4-pound whole chicken, free-range organic
- 7 tbsp olive oil, good quality olive oil
- 3 tbsp pepper, freshly ground is best
- 2 tbsp salt, kosher

Instructions

1. Preheat the cast-iron skillet while you prepare the chicken. Place the skillet in a 500 degree Fahrenheit oven and let the skillet heat!

2. Rub the entire chicken, front and back, legs, thighs… every inch with olive oil, salt, and pepper.

3. Remove the hot skillet from the oven to place the whole chicken in it.

4. Place the skillet and chicken back in the oven and cook for 15 minutes. The chicken will become a very nice dark, golden brown.

5. Lower the oven temperature to 350 degrees and cook the chicken for another 30-40 minutes until the chicken is a nice, golden, crispy brown color.

6. Use a meat thermometer to test the temperature, read more below.

7. The chicken is cooked when the thermometer reads 165 degrees Fahrenheit. You can remove it at 160 and it will continue to cook to 165.

8. Remove and let it sit for a minute. Spoon the juice on the bottom of the pan over the chicken.

Nutritional Value

Calories: 696kcal | Carbohydrates: 3g | Protein: 41g | Fat: 57g |

33. The Best Juicy Skillet Chicken Breasts

Prep Time: 10 mins Cook Time: 20 mins

Total Time: 30 mins

Ingredients

- 1 ½ pound boneless, skinless chicken breasts; 2 large breasts or 3 medium
- Salt, to taste
- 1 tsp. chili powder, see our homemade chili powder recipe
- 1 teaspoon garlic powder
- 1 teaspoon onion powder
- 1/2 teaspoon smoked paprika
- 1/2 teaspoon ground black pepper
- 1 Tbsp avocado oil or other high heat cooking oil
- Half of a lemon, quartered, optional

Instructions

1. Take the chicken out of the refrigerator and season on both sides with salt — we use just less than 1/4 tsp. of fine salt per chicken breast.

2. Make the spice rub by combining the chili powder, garlic powder, onion powder, smoked paprika, and black pepper. Liberally dust the spice rub all over the chicken.

3. Heat a tablespoon of oil in a medium frying pan (with lid) over medium-high heat. As soon as the oil is hot and looks shimmery, add the chicken. Cook 2 to 3 minutes until golden. Flip, reduce the heat to low and then splash a few Tbsp of water (or broth) into the skillet. Cover the skillet with a lid.

4. Cook 10 to 15 minutes or until an instant-read thermometer reads 165 degrees F when inserted into the thickest part of the breast.

5. Transfer the chicken to a plate and cover it loosely with aluminum foil. Let the chicken rest for 5 minutes, cut into thick slices, and then serve with pan drippings and lemon wedges.

Nutritional Value

Calories: 411kcal Total Fat: 4.6g| | Carbohydrate: 0.9g| | Protein: 38.5g

34. Easy Pan-Seared Chicken Breasts

Prep Time: 5 mins Cook Time: 10 mins

Total Time: 15 mins Serving: 4 Servings

Ingredients

- 4 chicken breasts (thin, boneless, and skinless)
- ½ cup flour
- 1 teaspoon sea salt
- ¼ teaspoon black pepper
- 1 tsp. garlic powder
- 1 teaspoon onion powder
- 2 teaspoons Italian seasoning
- 2 Tbsp olive oil

Instructions

1. Paper towel dry your thin chicken breasts (if you bought thick ones, make sure to butterfly each one). In a large bowl, combine flour, salt, black pepper, garlic powder, onion powder, and Italian Seasoning. Stir well to blend.
2. Using a fork or tongs, coat the chicken breasts in the flour mixture and set them aside.
3. Heat 2 Tbsp of olive oil in a large skillet over medium-high heat. Once the skillet is hot, place flour-coated chicken breasts in the skillet and cook for 4 to 5 minutes on each side, until golden brown on both sides and cooked through, turning once between cooking, about 8-10 minutes.
4. Remove chicken from pan and serve warm with pasta or vegetables.

Nutrition Facts

Calories: 347kcal Fat: 10g| |Carbohydrates: 13g| Protein: 25g

35. One Skillet Fiesta Chicken

Prep Time: 10 Mins Cook Time: 15 Mins

Total Time: 25 Mins Serving: 1-6 Servings

Ingredients

- 2 teaspoons extra-virgin olive oil
- 1 pound boneless skinless chicken breasts, cut into bite-size pieces
- 1/2 medium yellow onion or red onion, chopped
- 1 tablespoon garlic powder
- 2 tsp.s onion powder
- 1 1/2 teaspoons paprika
- 1 1/2 teaspoons dried dillweed
- 1/2 teaspoon cumin
- 1/2 teaspoon kosher salt
- 1/2 teaspoon cayenne pepper use 1/4 teaspoon
- 1 red bell pepper cored and chopped
- 1 green bell pepper cored and chopped
- 1 can black beans (15 ounces) rinsed and drained
- 1 can fire-roasted diced tomatoes in their juices
- 1 1/2 cups instant brown rice
- 1 cup low-sodium chicken stock
- 3/4 cup freshly grated cheddar cheese

Instructions

1. Heat the olive oil in a large nonstick skillet over medium-high heat.

2. Add the chicken, onion, garlic powder, onion powder, paprika, dill, salt, cumin, and cayenne pepper. Sauté, stirring often, for 3 minutes, until the chicken is beginning to brown on the outside.
3. Stir in the red bell pepper, green bell pepper, black beans, tomatoes, rice, and chicken stock.
4. Bring to a boil, and then cover and simmer on low heat for 5 minutes, or until the chicken is done and the rice is nearly tender.
5. Let stand, covered, for 5 minutes, until the liquid is absorbed.
6. Taste and adjust seasonings as desired. Sprinkle with cheese and any additional desired toppings.
7. Serve warm.

Nutritional Value

Calories: 329kcal| Carbohydrates: 41g| Protein: 27g| Fat: 8g

36. Crispy Cast Iron Skillet Chicken Thighs

Prep Time: 10 minutes Cook Time: 30 minutes

Total Time: 40 minutes Servings: 4 people

Ingredients

- 2 ½ lbs. about 6-8 bone-in, skin-on chicken thighs
- 1 teaspoon coarse salt
- 1 teaspoon garlic powder
- ½ tsp. freshly ground black pepper
- 1-2 Tbsp olive oil

Instructions

1. Heat oven to 425 degrees.
2. Pat the chicken thighs dry with a paper towel. In a small bowl, combine the salt, garlic powder, and pepper, then sprinkle over the meat on both sides.
3. In a cast-iron skillet, heat 1 to 2 Tbsp of olive oil over medium-high heat until hot. Place chicken thighs into the pan, skin side down, and cover with a splatter guard. Cook without moving for 7-9 minutes so that the fat can render and the skin can get nice and crispy.
4. Once the chicken releases from the pan and has a nicely browned crust on the skin, flip the chicken pieces overusing tongs.
5. Transfer the skillet with the chicken to the oven and roast for 18-20 minutes until cooked through and the internal temperature of the chicken reaches 165 degrees F when tested with an instant-read meat thermometer.

Nutrition Facts

Calories: 655kcal |Carbohydrates: 1g |Protein: 46g |Fat: 51g |

37. Cast-Iron Skillet Whole Roasted Chicken With Potatoes

Total Time: 1 hour 30 minutes Serving: 4 Servings

Ingredients

- 4 to 4 1/2 pound whole chicken
- Kosher salt
- Olive oil
- Freshly ground black pepper
- 1 onion any flavor will do, sliced
- 1 russet potato very thinly sliced (no need to peel the skin)
- 1/2 sweet potato very thinly sliced (no need to peel the skin)
- 6-8 sprigs of fresh thyme

Instructions

1. Pat the chicken dry with paper towels and season generously with kosher salt inside and out. Let the chicken sit for 1 hour, or in the refrigerator overnight.
2. Preheat the oven to 425°F and set a 12-inch cast-iron skillet inside on the middle rack. Tie the legs of the chicken together with string or twine and pat dry with paper towels again.
3. Drizzle with olive oil and lightly rub or brush the skin to cover it evenly. Season with a bit more salt and freshly ground black pepper. In a medium bowl, toss the vegetables with half of the thyme leaves and a drizzle of olive oil and set aside.
4. Once the oven comes to temperature, drizzle 1-2 Tbsp of oil in the skillet. Place the chicken in the hot pan and move out of the way in case the oil pops.
5. Carefully add the potatoes, onion, and thyme around the chicken and bake for 50-60 minutes or until a meat thermometer inserted into the thickest part of the thigh without touching the bone reads 155 to 160°F and the juices run clear.

6. Transfer from the oven and loosely tent with foil for about 15 minutes before serving.

Nutritional Value

Calories: 535kcal Protein: 38.3g| Carbohydrates: 72.7g|

38. Cast Iron Chicken Breast (Pan Roasted)

Prep Time: 10 Min Cook Time: 30 Min

Total Time: 40 Min Servings: 2

Ingredients

- 2 chicken breasts, bone-in, and skin-on
- 1/2 teaspoon kosher salt
- 1/4 tsp. black pepper, freshly cracked
- 1/4 teaspoon garlic powder
- 1 Tbsp ghee

Instructions

1. Preheat the oven to 450°F.
2. Pat chicken breasts dry with a paper towel
3. Combine 1/2 tsp. kosher salt, 1/4 tsp. pepper, and 1/4 tsp. garlic powder. Mix well.
4. Gently lift skin from the chicken breasts and sprinkle half the season mixture onto each breast under the skin. This will get the seasoning directly on the chicken meat.
5. Put the skin back in place.
6. Heat a 10" oven-safe cast-iron skillet over mid-high heat and melt 1 tablespoon ghee. Place the chicken breasts in the skillet with the skin side down and sear for 3-4 minutes
7. When chicken breasts are seared nicely, use tongs to flip them over
8. Place skillet in the preheated oven and cook for 25-30 minutes or until internal temperature reaches 162°F.
9. Use an instant-read thermometer to check the temperature in the thickest part of the chicken without touching the bone.
10. When the chicken breasts are cooked through, remove the skillet from the oven and allow the chicken to rest for 10 minutes

Nutritional Value

Calories: 455kcal Fat : 10.67g Carbs: 0.45g | Protein : 37.34| g

39. Crispy Skillet Chicken Thighs

Prep Time: 10 minutes Cook Time: 30 minutes

Total Time: 40 minutes Servings: 4

Ingredients

- 5-6 bone-in skin-on chicken thighs
- 2-3 Tbsp coconut oil
- 2 teaspoons kosher salt
- 1 teaspoon fresh ground pepper
- 2 tsp.s paprika
- 2 teaspoons granulated garlic

Instructions

1. Preheat oven to 425 degrees
2. In a small bowl mix salt, pepper, paprika, and granulated garlic.
3. With paper towels, pat the chicken dry, sprinkle seasoning on both sides of chicken thighs.
4. Heat a large cast-iron or oven-safe skillet to medium-high heat, add coconut oil, let melt.
5. Once the oil is hot, place chicken thighs skin side down in the hot skillet and cook, until skin is crispy about 8-10 minutes, flip chicken thighs and place skillet in the oven and cook another 15-18 minutes or until internal temp is 165 degrees.
6. Remove chicken and let the chicken rest 5 minutes before serving.

Nutrition Information

Calories: 378kcal Total Fat: 12g Carbohydrates: 2g| Protein: 15g

40. Roast Chicken With Vegetables

Prep Time: 25 Mins Cook Time: 70 Mins

Resting: 20 Mins Servings: 4 Servings

Ingredients

- 1 (4 to 4 1/2) pound chicken
- Kosher salt and freshly ground black pepper
- 6 cloves garlic, smashed and peeled (smash with the side of a chef's knife, makes it easier to peel)
- 6 sprigs thyme

• 3 medium rutabagas, peeled, trimmed, and cut into 1/4-inch wedges
• 2 medium turnips, peeled, trimmed, and cut into 1/4-inch wedges
• 4 medium carrots, peeled and cut into 2-inch segments
• 1 small yellow onion, peeled, roots trimmed but kept intact, cut into quarters
• 8 small red-skinned new potatoes
• 1/3 cup extra virgin olive oil, divided
• 4 Tbsp butter, room temperature (spreadable)

Method

1. Preheat The Oven: Preheat the oven to 475°F.
2. Cutaway The Wishbone: Use a paring knife to cut away the wishbone from the neck/breast area of the chicken. You will probably have to use your fingers to feel around for it. This is a little bit tricky, but if you can remove the wishbone first, it will make the chicken easier to carve after it is cooked. (This ease of future carving is the only reason to take the bone out, so you can leave it in if you want.)
3. Season The Cavity: Generously season the cavity of the chicken with salt and pepper. Add three of the garlic cloves and the sprigs of thyme to the cavity, using your hands to rub the thyme and garlic all around the cavity.
4. Truss The Chicken: Cut a 3-foot section of cotton kitchen string. Place the chicken so that it is breast up, and the legs pointing toward you. Tuck the wing tips under the chicken. Wrap the string under the neck end of the bird, pulling the string ends up over the breast, toward you, plumping up the breast. Then cross the string under the breast (above the cavity and between the legs). Wrap each end around the closest legend, and tie tightly so that the legs come together.
5. Toss The Vegetables With Olive Oil: Place the vegetables, onions, garlic, and remaining thyme sprig into a bowl. Add 1/4 cup of olive oil and toss with your hands until well coated. Season generously with salt and pepper. Create a bed of the root vegetables in a large cast-iron pan (or use a regular roasting pan if you don't have a cast-iron pan.) My father likes to leave out the potatoes at this stage and arrange them around the chicken.
6. Slather The Chicken With Oil And Season: Spread the remaining olive oil over the chicken skin. Season with salt and pepper.
7. Place the chicken in skillet: Place the chicken on the bed of vegetables. Slather the top of the chicken breasts with butter.
8. (Note that we added some extra sprigs of thyme to the top, probably because my dad forgot to add them to the vegetables! But it still worked.)
9. Roast In The Oven: Place the pan in the oven and roast the chicken for 25 minutes at 475°F. Then reduces the heat to 400°F and roast for an additional 45 minutes, or until the thickest part of the thigh registers 165°F on a meat thermometer and the juices run clear.
10. Cover And Let Rest On Cutting Board: Transfer the chicken to a cutting board, cover with aluminum foil and let rest for 20 minutes before carving to serve. You can keep the vegetables warm by keeping them in the now-turned-off oven while the chicken is resting. Stir to coat the vegetables with the cooking juices before serving
11. Cut The Chicken Into Serving Pieces: Place vegetables on a serving platter with the chicken pieces arranged on top.

Nutrition Facts

Calories: 425kcal Fat: 89g| Carbs: 136g| Protein: 139g

41. Dutch Oven Chicken

Prep Time: 15 min Cook Time: 60 min

Ready in Time: 75 min Servings: 4-6

Ingredients

• 2 lbs. gold potatoes
• 1 head of garlic
• 2 tbsp oil, divided
• 1 whole chicken
• 1¾ tsp salt, divided
• ¼ tsp paprika
• 1 lemon
• 3 sprigs fresh thyme

Instructions

1. Place the 6-qt. (5.7-L) Enameled Cast Iron Dutch Oven in the oven and preheat at 450°F.
2. Cut the potatoes into bite-sized pieces and place them in a bowl.
3. Remove 2 cloves of garlic from the head and press into the potatoes. Add 1 tbsp (15 mL) of oil and ½ tsp (2 mL) of salt; combine.
4. Cut off the wingtips and flats from the chicken
5. Brush the chicken with the remaining oil; season with paprika and the remaining salt.
6. Cut the head of garlic and the lemon in half horizontally; place in the cavity of the chicken with the thyme. Tie the legs together with kitchen twine.
7. Carefully remove the Dutch oven from the oven. Add the potatoes to the bottom and place the chicken on top. Replace the lid.
8. Bake, covered, for 45 minutes. Remove the lid and bake until the skin is browned, and the chicken reaches 165°F (74°C), about 15–20 minutes.

Nutrients Value

Calories: 429kcal Total Fat: 15g| Carbohydrate: 27g| | Protein: 38g

42. Marinated Spatchcock Chicken In Cast Iron

Prep Time: 10 Minutes Cook Time: 40 Minutes

Total Time: 50 Minutes Servings: 4

Ingredients

For the chicken

- 2 Tbsp (30 ml) olive oil
- 4 cloves garlic, roughly chopped
- ½ teaspoon herbes de Provence
- 1 teaspoon fine sea salt
- ¼ tsp. freshly ground black pepper
- Zest of 1 lemon
- 2 Tbsp (30 ml) freshly squeezed lemon juice
- 1 good-quality whole chicken (about 4 pounds/1800 grams), spatchcocked

Instructions

1. Preheat the oven to 425°F with a rack in the center.
2. To make the. marinade, place the olive oil, garlic, herbs, salt, and pepper into a mortar. Zest the lemon directly into the mortar, and add the lemon juice.
3. Bash the mixture with the pestle, crushing the garlic against the sides and bottom, to form a rough, chunky marinade.
4. Dry the chicken well with paper towels and place it skin-side-up in a 12-inch cast-iron skillet.
5. Pour the marinade over top and use your hands to distribute it evenly over the chicken.
6. At this point, you can roast right away or leave the chicken to marinate at room temperature for 30 minutes or in the fridge for up to 24 hours.
7. Roast for about 40 minutes depending on size until the juices run clear when you insert a knife between a leg and thigh, and breast meat reads 150°F on an instant thermometer.
8. Let the chicken rest for at least 10 minutes before carving.
9. If you'd like to make gravy, set the skillet over medium heat while the chicken rests. Whisk the flour into the pan drippings.
10. When incorporated, pour in the broth and whisk until smooth.
11. Bring to a boil, then simmer for five minutes until thickened. (You can adjust the amount of broth to suit your preference.)
12. Whisk in the soy sauce and marmite and serve.

Nutritional Value

Calories: 529kcal Total Fat: 29g| Carbohydrates: 8g| Protein: 45g

43. Pan Seared Oven Baked Chicken Breast

Prep Time: 10 minutes Cook Time: 20 minutes

Total Time: 30 minutes Servings: 4

Ingredients

- 2 skinless boneless chicken breasts - about 10 oz each well-timed
- 1 tsp. oil
- Salt and pepper to taste

Instructions

1. Preheat the oven to 375° convection (400° for a regular oven).

2. Put an oven-safe pan on a stovetop over medium-high heat with a teaspoon of oil. I use a 10 inch cast iron skillet. Trim and pat dry the chicken

3. Sprinkle lightly with salt and pepper or seasoning of your choice.

4. When the oil is hot and shimmering, carefully lay the chicken breasts in the hot pan. Brown both sides for 3-4 minutes each.

5. Get them to almost the color you want when eating. So you have seared, flipped, seared, flipped, and then to the oven.

6. Bake for 15-20 minutes until an internal temperature of 165°. The thinner breast will be 15 minutes and the thicker bigger ones for about 20 minutes.

7. Let rest for 5 minutes before serving. Done in less than 30 minutes, and you spent most of the time setting and unwinding. Not bad, not bad at all.

Nutritional Value

Calories : 220 kcal| Protein : 48g| Fat : 4g|

44. Cast-Iron Skillet Chicken Thighs

Servings: 2-4 Prep Time: 5 Minutes

Cook Time: 32 Minutes

Ingredients

- 6 skin-on, bone-in chicken thighs (about 2 1/4 pounds)
- Kosher salt and freshly ground pepper
- 1 Tbsp vegetable oil

Instructions

1. Preheat oven to 475°. Season chicken with salt and pepper.

2. Heat oil in a 12" cast-iron or heavy nonstick skillet over high heat until hot but not smoking.

3. Nestle chicken in skillet, skin side down, and cook 2 minutes.

4. Reduce heat to medium-high; continue cooking skin side down, occasionally rearranging chicken thighs and rotating pan to evenly distribute heat, until fat renders and skin is golden brown, about 12 minutes.

5. Transfer skillet to oven and cook 13 more minutes.

6. Flip chicken; continue cooking until skin crisps and meat is cooked through, about 5 minutes longer.

7. Transfer to a plate; let rest 5 minutes before serving.

Nutritional Value

Calories: 689kcal | Carbohydrates: 36.8g | Protein: 70.8g | Fat: 28.2g |

45. Skillet Roasted Chicken Recipe

Prep Time: 3 Mins Cook Time: 25 Mins

Servings: 6

Ingredients

- 1-2 Tbsp olive oil
- 6-8 chicken thighs skin on
- Salt and pepper
- 1 teaspoon paprika
- 6 whole garlic cloves peeled
- Fresh thyme sprigs

Instructions

1. Preheat oven to 475° degrees.

2. Heat 12-inch cast-iron skillet over medium-high heat on stove or cooktop. Drizzle in olive oil and heat, but do not overheat to allow it to smoke.

3. Sprinkle salt and pepper on chicken thighs and place the chicken skin side down into the skillet. Cook 2 minutes or until chicken skin has browned. Turn and reduce heat to medium.

4. Cook chicken until the fat has rendered off, about 10-12 more minutes.

5. Sprinkle chicken with paprika, nestle in whole garlic cloves throughout chicken thighs, and top with thyme sprigs.
6. Place in oven and roast until chicken temperature registers 160° F when checked with an internal temperature probe, about 12-13 more minutes.
7. Remove from oven and allow to rest for about 5 minutes.

Nutritional Information

Calories: 274kcal | Carbohydrates: 1g | Protein: 19g | Fat: 21g |

46. Creamy Chicken And Mushroom Skillet

Prep Time: 15 mins Cook Time: 25 mins

Total Time: 40 mins Servings: 8

Ingredients

- 8 boneless skinless chicken thighs or 4 chicken breasts
- 1/2 cup all-purpose flour seasoned with 1 teaspoon salt and 1/4 teaspoon pepper
- 2 Tbsp butter 1 Tbsp for chicken, 1 tablespoon for mushrooms
- 1 Tbsp olive oil
- 8 ounces sliced cremini mushrooms
- 3 clove large garlic chopped
- 1 1/2 cups chicken stock or white wine or a combo of both. Beef stock can also be substituted
- 1/2 cup heavy cream see notes if subbing half and half
- 2 Tbsp dijon mustard
- 1 Tbsp heaping chopped fresh thyme or 2 teaspoons dry
- 1/2 cup asiago cheese or other hard cheese like Parmesan

Instructions

1. Heat large skillet to medium-high heat. Add 1 Tbsp each of butter and olive oil.
2. Place seasoned flour on a plate. Dredge chicken in flour and place in a hot skillet. Sear on each side until crispy brown. About 4 minutes on each side
3. Removed seared chicken to plate and set aside. Reduce heat to medium. Add one Tbsp of butter to the skillet along with mushrooms. Saute for a few minutes until mushrooms are slightly brown.
4. Add garlic and thyme. Continue to cook for another minute until the garlic is soft and fragrant.
5. Add stock (or wine) to the pan scraping up all the bits on the bottom of the pan.
6. Add cream, dijon, and cheese. Stir until creamy and combined.
7. Taste for seasoning with salt and pepper
8. Add chicken back to the pan and simmer for another 10-12 minutes or until internal temp of chicken reaches 165 degrees and gravy is reduced by a third and covers the back of a spoon.
9. Serve with rice or potatoes and a simple salad or steamed veggies!

Nutrition Facts

Calories: 329kcal Fat: 34g| Saturated Fat: 16g|: 20g| Protein: 55g|

47. Lemon Chicken

Prep Time: 15 mins Cook Time: 1 hr

Total Time: 1 hr 15 mins Servings: 4

Ingredients

- Roasted lemon chicken
- 1 whole roasting chicken butterflied
- 2 large lemons sliced thick
- 1 large yellow onion sliced thick
- 4 Tbsp extra virgin olive oil
- 4 Tbsp butter
- 1 tsp. mccormick "grill mates" brown sugar bourbon or lemon pepper
- Salt and black pepper to taste
- ½ cup dry white wine
- Lemon slices for garnish if desired

Instructions

1. Roasted Lemon Chicken
2. Simply give the pan a good brushing off a few Tbsp of either extra virgin olive oil or canola oil. Then layer 2 large lemons, sliced thick in the bottom of the pan, along with a large onion, sliced. Ask your butcher to butterfly the chicken, so it will lay fairly flat in the pan.

3. Place the butterflied chicken on top of the lemon and onion slices. Melt 4 Tbsp of butter and drizzle along with 4 Tbsp or so of extra virgin olive oil over the chicken. Sprinkle with salt, black pepper, and 1 teaspoon of McCormick "Grill Mates" brown sugar bourbon seasoning over top the chicken.
4. Cook in a preheated 400 degree F oven for 40 minutes. Then takes out and pour ½ cup of dry white wine around the chicken. Place the pan back in the oven for about another 15-20 minutes. Or until the chicken is thoroughly cooked and has an internal temperature of 165 degrees F.
5. Let the chicken rest for 5 to 10 minutes before slicing. This chicken is super moist and pairs well with a glass of white wine. Try it served over rice pilaf and seasonal vegetables.

Nutrition Facts

Calories: 692kcal | Carbohydrates: 10g | Protein: 37g | Fat: 54g

48. One Pan-roasted Chicken And Potatoes

Prep Time: 10 minutes Cook Time: 35 minutes

Total Time: 45 minutes Servings: 3

Ingredients

- 1 pound bone-in skin-on chicken breasts
- 2 Tbsp olive oil divided
- 1½ tsp. Kosher salt divided
- 1 teaspoon freshly ground black pepper divided
- 1 tsp. Italian seasoning
- ½ medium onion sliced
- 1 large carrot rough chopped
- 1 stalk celery rough chopped
- 1.5 pounds baby gold potatoes halved

Pan Sauce

- 1 cup low sodium chicken stock divided
- 1 Tbsp butter
- 1 teaspoon cornstarch
- 1-2 Tbsp water
- 1 Tablespoon fresh parsley chopped, plus additional for garnish
- 1 teaspoon fresh thyme chopped

Instructions

1. Preheat your oven to 425°F.
2. Drizzle the chicken with 1 Tbsp of olive oil then season on all sides with 1 tsp. of Kosher salt, ½ tsp. of ground pepper, and 1 teaspoon of Italian seasoning.
3. Heat a 12 inch cast-iron skillet over medium-high heat. Add 1 Tbsp of oil and swirl to coat the pan, then place the chicken breasts on the skin side down.
4. Sear the chicken for around 3 minutes until the skin is browned, then flip and cook for another minute. Be careful not to burn the skin.
5. Remove the skillet from the heat and transfer the chicken to a plate.
6. Add the chopped carrot, celery, and onion to the pan, then place the seared chicken breasts on top.
7. Cut the potatoes in half and toss with 1 Tbsp of olive oil, 1 teaspoon of Kosher salt, and ½ teaspoon of ground pepper.
8. Arrange the potatoes around the chicken and place the pan in the oven. Bake for 25-30 minutes until the chicken reaches an internal temperature of 165°F and the potatoes are cooked through.
9. Transfer the chicken and potatoes to a platter and tent loosely with foil to keep warm. Discard the onion, carrots, and celery but do not wipe the pan.

Pan Sauce

1. Set the skillet over medium-high heat and add ¼ cup of the chicken stock. Scrape up any brown bits from the pan. Stir in the remaining stock and butter and bring to a low simmer.
2. Once the butter has melted, stir together the cornstarch and water in a small bowl then whisk into the stock. Simmer until slightly thickened, around 2 minutes.
3. Season with salt and pepper to taste and stir in fresh chopped parsley and thyme, then spoon over the chicken and garnish with additional chopped parsley before serving.

Nutrition Facts

Calories: 406kcal| Carbohydrates: 42g| Protein: 34g| Fat: 18g|

49. Spatchcock Cast-Iron Mustard Chicken

Prep Time: 20 mins Cook Time: 35 mins

Total Time: 55 mins Servings 4

Ingredients

- 1 whole Chicken
- 4 lb. chicken spatchcocked
- 6-8 garlic cloves minced
- 3 Tbsp Dijon mustard
- 3 Tbsp whole grain mustard
- 2 Tbsp avocado oil
- 1 tablespoon coconut amigos soy sauce
- 1 tsp. hot sauce I use Valentina
- 1 Tbsp herbes de Provence
- 1 teaspoon red pepper flakes

Instructions

1. Preheat to 450F.
2. Mix all the ingredients (except the chicken) in a bowl.
3. Put 2 Tbsp of the mixture under the skin of each breast. Put 2 Tbsp of the mixture under the skin of each thigh.
4. Heat your cast-iron skillet on the stove. Add a thin layer of oil, if necessary*. Add ¼ of the remaining mixture to the non-skin side of each chicken half and place the chicken skin side up in the pan. Add the remaining mixture on top of the chicken. Cook 5 minutes until starts to brown. Transfer to the oven.
5. Cook 30-35 minutes in the oven until the internal temperature reads 155F when checking the inside of the chicken breast.* It will continue to cook while it rests. Let rest 5 minutes before serving.

Nutritional Value

Calories: 1067kcal | Carbohydrates: 4g | Protein: 86g | Fat: 76g

50. Skillet Chicken With Apples And Onions

Prep Time: 15 minutes Cook Time: 30 minutes

Total Time: 45 minutes Servings: 4

Ingredients

- 4 boneless skinless chicken cutlets (about 6 ounces each)
- ½ cup all-purpose flour, for dredging
- Kosher salt and pepper, to taste
- 1 Tbsp olive oil
- 2 Tbsp butter
- ½ of a sweet onion, thinly sliced
- 2 medium apples, sliced (I like a firm-flesh apple such as Granny Smith, Honey Crisp, Pink Lady, or Braeburn)
- 2 cloves garlic, pressed or minced
- 1 tablespoon minced fresh rosemary
- 1 cup chicken broth
- ¼ - ½ cup heavy cream, at room temperature
- 2 Tbsp Dijon mustard
- 1 teaspoon brown sugar (or sub with maple syrup)

Instructions

1. Pat chicken dry and season on all sides with salt and pepper.
2. Place the flour in a shallow dish and season with salt and pepper. Dredge each chicken cutlet in the seasoned flour, shaking off any excess flour.
3. In a large skillet, heat olive oil over medium-high heat. Stir in butter.
4. When the butter is foamy, add the chicken cutlets to the pan. Cook until the chicken is browned on both sides and the meat reaches an internal temperature of 165° F, about 3-4 minutes per side. Do not overcrowd the pan, so brown the chicken in batches if necessary.
5. Remove the chicken to a plate and set it aside while you make the sauce.
6. Add the sliced onion and apples to the skillet and cook over medium-high heat until the onion is translucent about 5 minutes. Add the garlic and rosemary; cook, stirring constantly, for 30 seconds.
7. Add the chicken broth to the skillet; use a wooden spoon to scrape up any browned bits from the bottom of the pan. Simmer for 3-4 minutes, so that the liquid reduces by about half.
8. Reduce heat to low, gradually whisk in the cream, Dijon, and brown sugar. start with about ¼ cup of cream, and then slowly add more, if desired. Cook for a few more minutes to let the sauce thicken (do not boil). Taste and season with salt and pepper. Return chicken to the skillet; garnish with additional fresh herbs. Serve immediately.

Nutrition Value

Calories: 502kcal | Carbohydrates: 29g | Protein: 39g | Fat: 25g |

RED MEAT RECIPES

51. One Skillet Beef Tips With Peppers And Onions

Prep Time: 10 Minutes Cook Time: 20 Minutes

Total Time: 30 Minutes Servings: 4

Ingredients

- 1 ½ tbsp Avocado Oil
- 1 pound sirloin steak, cut into small bite-sized pieces
- 2 tsp salt
- ½ tsp black pepper
- 1 tbsp apple cider vinegar
- 3 cloves garlic, minced
- 1 red bell pepper, diced into large chunks
- 1 orange bell pepper, diced into large chunks
- ½ yellow onion, sliced
- 1 ½ cups sliced mushrooms
- ¼ cup sliced green onion, for garnish

Method

1. Add the steak to a mixing bowl and season with salt and pepper. Stir until well combined.
2. Heat a large skillet over medium-high heat. Once the skillet is hot, you can add in the ghee.
3. Next, add the steak bites to the skillet cook for 3-5 minutes until browned on all sides. Remove the meat from the pan and set it aside.
4. Add the apple cider vinegar to the skillet to deglaze the pan. Then, add the minced garlic, onion, mushrooms, and diced peppers.
5. Cook the veggies for 10-12 more minutes until the sliced onion is translucent and the bell peppers are tender yet crisp.
6. Add the steak and its juices back to the skillet. When the beef is back in the pan, give everything a good stir until well combined and cook for 2-3 more minutes until the steak is hot.
7. Remove the skillet from the heat and garnish with fresh sliced green onion before serving.

Nutritional Value

Calories Per Serving: 235

52. Cast Iron Skillet Steak

Prep Time: 5 minutes Cook Time: 12 minutes

Servings: 2

Ingredients

- 16 ounces ribeye steak
- 4 Tbsp unsalted butter
- 5 garlic cloves
- 4 sprigs of fresh rosemary
- kosher salt
- freshly ground pepper

Instructions

1. Place a deep cast-iron skillet over medium-high heat.
2. Once the skillet is hot, pat the steak dry one more time - just removing any moisture, not the seasoning.
3. Then place the steak in the hot pan.
4. After about 3-4 minutes, a nice crust should form on the steak, flip it over for another 3-4 minutes and check the temperature. If steak has not reached the desired temperature, keep flipping it over and checking the temperature every 2 minutes or so. Total cook time will depend on the thickness of the steak.
5. Just before steak reaches the desired temperature, add butter, garlic, and rosemary to the pan.
6. Let rosemary and garlic sizzle in the butter for a bit. Then carefully tip the pan toward you so the butter pools, and spoon it over the steak a few times.
7. Remove the steak from the hot pan and allow to rest for 5 minutes before slicing and serving.

Nutrition Fact

Calories: 684kcal | Carbohydrates: 3g | Protein: 46g | Fat: 55g

53. Beef Tips And Gravy

Prep Time: 15 mins Cook Time: 3 hours

Total Time: 3 hours 15 mins Servings: 6 servings

Ingredients

- 2 lbs boneless beef chuck
- Kosher salt
- Ground pepper
- 1/4 cup vegetable oil, divided
- 1 yellow onion, diced
- 2 stalks of celery, diced
- 1 carrot, diced
- 4 cloves garlic, minced
- 2 Tbsp tomato paste
- 1/4 cup all-purpose flour
- 3 cups beef stock
- 1 bay leaf
- 3 sprigs of thyme
- 3 stems of Italian parsley
- 1 tablespoon red wine vinegar
- 3 Tbsp minced Italian parsley

Instructions

1. Cut the beef chuck into small strips, about 1 to 2-inches in length and 1/4-inch thick. Season generously with salt and pepper.
2. Preheat a large cast-iron skillet over medium-high heat. Add 2 Tbsp of the oil and swirl to coat the skillet.
3. Add half of the beef and cook, turning halfway through, until browned on both sides, 5-6 minutes.
4. Use a slotted spoon to remove the beef from the skillet into a bowl, then sear the remaining half of the beef.
5. Decrease the heat to medium and add the remaining 2 Tbsp of oil.
6. Add the onion and cook until it starts to soften, then add the celery and carrot and continue to cook, stirring often, until softened, about 5 minutes.
7. Add the garlic and cook for 30 seconds, then stir in the tomato paste.
8. Add the flour and stir through, until no dry flour remains.
9. Slowly start whisking in the beef stock. Bring to a boil, stirring constantly and scraping up all of the browned bits from the bottom of the skillet.
10. Reduce the heat to medium-low. Return the beef to the skillet, along with any juices that have accumulated.
11. Add the bay leaf, thyme, and stems of parsley. Put a lid on the skillet and simmer, stirring occasionally, until the sauce has thickened and the beef is tender, 2 1/4 to 2 1/2 hours. If needed, cook uncovered the last half hour to get to your desired thickness.
12. Discard the bay leaf, thyme, and parsley stems.
13. Stir in the red wine vinegar and minced parsley. Season to taste with salt and pepper.
14. Serve hot.

Nutrition Fact

Calories: 478| Sugar: 2g| Sodium: 520mg| Fat: 35g| Saturated Fat: 12g

54. Cheesy Ground Beef Skillet Pasta Recipe

Prep Time: 10 minutes Cook Time: 40 minutes

Total Time: 50 minutes Servings: 4

Ingredients

- 8 ounces (1/2 a box) medium pasta, such as malloreddus, shells, or rotini
- 1 to 2 Tbsp extra-virgin olive oil
- 1 pound ground beef, preferably grass-fed
- 1 teaspoon garlic powder
- 1/2 teaspoon crushed red pepper flakes
- Kosher salt and ground black pepper
- One 20-ounce jar pasta sauce
- 8 ounces (about 2 cups) shredded sharp cheddar cheese

Instructions

1. Heat the oven to 400°F.
2. Cook the pasta per the instructions on the box in a large pot of boiling salted water until al dente; drain.
3. Meanwhile, heat the oil in a large cast-iron skillet over medium heat. Add the ground beef and season with garlic powder, crushed red pepper flakes, and some salt and pepper, and cook, breaking apart with a wooden spoon until the beef is cooked through 5 to 7 minutes.
4. Add the pasta sauce and simmer, reducing the heat as needed, for 15 minutes. Taste and adjust the seasonings to your liking.
5. Add the cooked pasta along with one-quarter (about 1/2 cup) of the cheese to the sauce and stir to combine.

Sprinkle the remaining cheese on top and bake in the oven until the cheese has melted and the sauce is gently bubbling about 15 minutes. Let cool slightly before serving.

Nutritional Value

Calories: 423 Carbohydrates: 29g | Protein: 39g | Fat: 25g |

55. Potato, Beef Tips, And Gravy Skillet

Prep: 15 mins Cook: 30 mins

Total: 45 mins Servings: 4 servings

Ingredients

- 1 Tbsp oil
- 1 pound beef tips
- 1 large onion chopped
- 2 large carrots diced
- ½ pound mushrooms quartered
- 1 Tbsp tomato paste
- ¼ cup red wine or use water
- 2 Tbsp flour
- ½ teaspoon salt
- Black pepper to taste
- 2.5 cups beef stock
- 1 bay leaf optional
- 1.5 pounds baby potatoes diced
- 1 Tbsp cornstarch stirred into 3 Tbsp water to make a slurry

Instructions

1. Heat the oil in a large skillet over medium-high heat. Add the beef and cook about 30 seconds on either side, until browned.

2. Reduce the heat to medium. Add the onion and carrots to the skillet and stir well. Allow to cook for 2-3 minutes, then add the mushrooms and cook until they're starting to soften.

3. Stir the tomato paste into the skillet and cook for 30 seconds, then pour in the red wine. Allow the wine to cook away before sprinkling the flour over the beef and vegetables. Stir it in very well, until no white spots remain.

4. Pour the stock into the skillet and stir well. Season with salt and pepper and add the bay leaf, if using. Allow coming to a boil before stirring in the potatoes. Reduce the heat to medium-low and allow the skillet to simmer for 10-15 minutes or until the potatoes are done.

5. Finally, stir the cornstarch slurry into the skillet and simmer until gravy has thickened. Double the cornstarch if you like a thick gravy.

Nutrition

Calories: 494 Carbohydrates: 44.71g| Protein: 31.05g| Fat: 17.16g|

56. Cast Iron Flank Steak

Prep Time: 10 mins Cook Time: 10 mins

Total Time: 20 mins Servings: 4

Ingredients

- 1/2 cup olive oil
- 1/3 cup soy sauce
- 1/4 cup red wine vinegar
- 1 tbsp minced garlic
- 2 tbsp honey
- 1 tsp black pepper
- 1 1/2 to 2 lbs flank steak or skirt steak

Instructions

1. Whisk olive oil, soy sauce, vinegar, garlic, pepper, and honey until the honey dissolves and becomes a uniform marinade.
2. Place meat in a shallow dish and pour marinade over meat coating it thoroughly. Cover and refrigerate overnight or for whatever amount of time you have available.
3. Preheat a large cast-iron pan to medium-high heat on top of the stove.
4. Place steak in the cast iron pan for approximately 4 minutes. Flip the steak to the other side.
5. Look for pink beads of moisture to appear on the steak - that is a good indicator of medium-rare.
6. Cook 3-4 minutes and remove. Let steak stand for 5 minutes before slicings thinly.

Nutrition Facts

Calories: 354 Fat: 24g| Carbohydrates: 7g| Protein: 26g|

57. Beef And Red Wine Stew With Dumplings

Prep Time: 25 Mins Cook Time: 2 Hrs 30 Mins

Total Time: 2 Hrs 55 Mins Servings: 4

Ingredients

Beef Stew Ingredients

- 2 tbsp Plain flour
- 1.2 lb Stewing steak aka diced beef, braising steak or chuck steak
- salt and pepper
- 3 tbsp Olive Oil 2 tbsp for the beef and 1 tbsp for the vegetables
- 2 Onions diced
- 2 large Carrots chopped
- 10 oz Swede chopped into cubes
- 2 cups Beef Stock
- 1 cup Red Wine
- 7 oz Chestnut mushrooms chopped
- 1 tsp Worcestershire sauce
- 2 Bay leaf
- 3 sprigs Thyme sprigs (fresh) sub with 1tsp dried thyme

Dumpling Ingredients

- 1 ½ cups self-raising flour
- 7 tbsp butter, margarine, fat, or vegetable shortening
- 6 sprigs thyme only leaves needed or with 1 tsp dried thyme
- 10 tbsp water
- salt and pepper to taste

Instructions

Beef Stew

- Preheat the oven 150° / 300°F fan oven.
- Sprinkle diced beef with plain flour and season with salt and pepper.
- Chunks of stewing steak covered in plain flour and black pepper in a white and blue bowl
- Heat the 2 tbsp of olive oil, in a cast-iron dish/casserole dish on high heat. Add the stewing steak and sear until just browned on all sides.
- Browning off chuck steak cubes in a grey cast iron pan
- Don't worry about bits that have stuck to the bottom of the dish we will soak these up later.
- Remove the cooked steak and place it to one side in a bowl.
- Leftover fat and dregs of browned flour on the cast iron pan after browning off the chunks of stewing steak ready for deglazing
- Add 1 more tbsp of oil with the onions, carrots, and swede to the pan and cook for 8 mins.
- Chopped onion, carrots, and swede in a cast iron pan ready to cook
- Next, add the mushrooms for 2 mins.
- Mushrooms added to the cast iron pan with the chopped onion, carrots, and swede
- Push the vegetables to the sides and pour the red wine into the center of the pan.
- The wine will loosen the stuck bits off the bottom gathering all the flavors and flour ready for thickening your casserole. This is known as deglazing.
- Pouring red wine into the middle of the cast iron pan with the chopped mushrooms, swede, carrots, and onions
- Add beef stock and bring to the boil
- Pouring beef stock into the cast iron pan with the chopped mushrooms, swede, carrots, and onions

- Add Worcestershire sauce and return the beef to the pan
- Pouring in a teaspoon of Worcestershire sauce into the beef stock mixture with chopped onions, swede, mushrooms, and carrots
- Finally, add the thyme sprigs and bay leaves.
- Stewing beef chunks, thyme sprigs, and bay leaves have been added to the stew cooking in a cast iron pan
- Put the lid on and transfer to the 150°C / 300°F oven for 2 hrs.
- Placing the lid on the cast iron pan to cook the beef stew in the oven

How To Make Dumplings

- Place all the plain flour, beef suet, thyme leaves, salt, and pepper in a large mixing bowl.
- Self-raising flour, beef suet, and thyme leaves in a large silver bowl
- Add cold water and mix with your hands until the mixture forms a sticky dough
- Mixing the dumpling mix by hands in a large silver bowl
- Roll into 8, slightly larger than golf ball-sized balls
- Rolling out a dumpling by hands
- Take the casserole dish out after 2 hours, remove the bay leaves and thyme sprigs.
- Place the dumplings on top of the stew and push them down halfway into the liquid.
- Replace the lid on the dish and put it back in the oven for 20 mins.
- Pushing the dumplings into our Beef and Red Wine Stew in a cast iron pan
- If you want a crispy top take the lid off and cook for a final 10 minutes.
- If you prefer soft dumplings keep a lid on for another 10 minutes.
- Beef and Red Wine Stew with Dumplings in a cast iron pan
- Sprinkle with some more fresh thyme and you are ready to serve!
- Beef and Red Wine Stew with Dumplings in a cast iron pan served on a wooden board with a bowl of garden peas garnished with butter, sprinkled sprigs of thyme, a large wooden spoon on the side, and green and flowery cloth in the background

Nutrition Value

Calories: 766kcal| Carbohydrates: 43g| Protein: 37g| Fat: 45g|

58. Cast-Iron Coulotte With Chimichurri Sauce

Prep Time: 5 minutes Cook Time: 20 minutes

Total Time: 25 minutes Servings: 4 Servings

Ingredients

- 1 pkg butcherbox Coulotte/Top Sirloin Cap
- Salt
- Pepper
- 1 Tbsp avocado oil preferred oil: Primal Kitchen Avocado Oil
- Chimichurri Sauce
- 4 cloves garlic minced
- 2 Tbsp butter
- 1 Tbsp red wine vinegar approximate
- Parsley handful
- Cilantro handful

Instructions

1. Pre-heat oven to 425°F.
2. Season meat with salt and pepper on both sides.
3. Put oil in the skillet and pre-heat skillet on the stovetop. Make sure the skillet is hot. Place meat with the fat cap side down and let it sear for 2 - 3 minutes without moving it.
4. Turn meat and place skillet in the oven and cook for 15 minutes until the meat has reached 120°F. Let meat rest on a countertop.
5. Discard some of the oil and reserve it for later. Add the garlic and cook for 1 minute. Be sure not to burn your garlic.
6. Deglaze the pan with vinegar. Follow with adding butter and herbs, and then place the meat back in the pan.
7. Baste the meat with sauce by leaning the pan to one side and letting the juices slide to one side and spooning the liquid onto the meat.
8. After 2 minutes, take your meat out of the pan and slice against the grain.

Nutrition Information

Calories: 766 kcal Total Fat: 12gCarbohydrates: 2g| Protein: 15g

59. Cheesy Nacho Beef Skillet

Prep Time: 10 Mins Total Time: 30 Mins

Servings: 6

Ingredients

- 1 lb lean (at least 80%) ground beef
- 1 pouch (8 oz) Old El Paso™ Mexican rice
- 2 cans (10 oz each) diced tomatoes with green chiles
- 1 can (15.25 oz) whole kernel sweet corn
- 1 package (1 oz) Old El Paso™ taco seasoning mix
- 1 roasted red bell pepper (from a jar), chopped
- 1/2 cup water
- 1 1/2 cups shredded Mexican cheese blend (6 oz)

Instructions

1. In a 10-inch skillet, cook 1 lb lean ground beef over medium-high heat until thoroughly cooked, stirring frequently; drain.
2. Meanwhile, microwave 1 pouch (8 oz) Old El Paso Mexican rice as directed on pouch.
3. To skillet with cooked beef, add 2 cans (10 oz each) diced tomatoes with green chiles, 1 can (15.25 oz) whole kernel sweet corn, 1 package (1 oz) Old El Paso™ taco seasoning mix, 1 roasted red bell pepper (from a jar), chopped, and 1/2 cup water; mix well.
4. Stir in cooked Mexican rice. Heat to boiling. Reduce heat; simmer for 10 minutes.
5. Stir in 1 cup shredded Mexican cheese blend until melted. Sprinkle the remaining 1/2 cup cheese over top. Serve immediately.

Nutrition Information

Calories: 400| Total Fat: 19g, Protein: 23g| Total Carbohydrate: 32g|

60. Beef Bourguignon

Prep Time: 20 minutes Cook Time: 1 hour 30 minutes

Total Time: 1 hour 50 minutes Servings: 4

Ingredients

- 2 1/2 pounds boneless beef chuck trimmed and cut into 1-inch cubes
- 1/2 tsp. kosher salt
- 1/2 teaspoon freshly ground black pepper
- 1/4 cup all-purpose flour
- 8 ounces bacon diced
- 1 yellow onion diced
- 6 carrots diced
- 4 celery stalks diced
- 1 pound cremini or button mushroom sliced
- 4 cloves garlic pressed or minced
- 1/2 cup cognac
- 1 Tbsp tomato paste
- 2 cups dry red wine such as Pinot Noir
- 2 cups beef stock
- 1 Tbsp brown sugar
- 1 teaspoon fresh thyme leaves
- Chopped fresh Italian parsley for garnish

Instructions

1. Preheat the oven to 350°F.
2. Add the beef to a large mixing bowl and season it with salt and pepper then toss with the flour. Set aside.
3. In a large cast-iron cocotte dutch oven, cook the bacon over medium-low heat until the edges of the bacon are crispy. Remove the bacon to a large bowl, leaving the rendered fat in the pan.
4. Increase the heat to medium-high. Add the beef to the fat in the pan and brown it on all sides. Remove the beef from the pan to the bowl with the bacon.
5. Add the onions, carrots, celery, and mushrooms to the pan. Reduce the heat to medium and cook for 5 to 7

minutes, until softened. Add the garlic and cook for another minute, or until aromatic. Remove the vegetables from the pan to the bowl with the beef.

6. Deglaze the pan with the cognac and cook until reduced by half, scraping the bottom of the pan to release any browned bits.

7. Stir in the tomato paste then add the wine, stock, thyme, brown sugar, and a big pinch of salt and pepper. Bring to a boil, then remove from the heat.

8. Return the bacon, beef, and vegetable stop the pot, cover, and place in the oven.

9. Cook for 1 1/2 to 2 hours in the preheated oven, until the beef is fork-tender. Remove from the oven, and adjust the seasoning if needed.

10. Serve garnished with parsley over my favorite mashed potatoes or mashed cauliflower.

Nutrition Value

Calories: 527kcal | Carbohydrates: 16g | Protein: 35g | Fat: 28g |

61. Skillet Steak Bites Recipe

Prep Time: 10 Mins Cook Time: 10 Mins

Total Time: 20 Mins Servings: 4

Ingredients

- 1 lb beef sirloin or tenderloin steak
- Salt and pepper
- 1 tbsp unsalted butter
- 1/4 cup dry red wine
- 2 tsp worcestershire sauce

Instructions

1. Cut beef into ¾ cubes and trim away any excess fat or gristle. Season steak cubes lightly with salt and pepper. Remember, the sauce will also contain the salt from Worcestershire sauce.

2. Heat a large heavy-bottom skillet, preferably cast iron, over medium-high heat and allow it to become very hot. Add 1 Tbsp butter and swirl the pan to melt butter and coat the bottom of the pan. Immediately scatter half of the seasoned steak cubes evenly across the bottom of the pan and allow it to cook, undisturbed, for about 1 minute before stirring to cook on other sides.

3. Continue cooking, stirring occasionally for 2–3 minutes or until browned on most sides then transfer to a plate. If you prefer your meat well done, just leave it in the pan a bit longer until cooked through. Add a second batch of meat and cook in the same manner, adding a bit more butter if necessary.

4. Once all meat has been removed from the skillet, return the skillet to heat and add red wine and Worcestershire sauce. Allow the liquid to bubble and reduce until only about 1 Tbsp remains. Remove from heat and add remaining ½ tsp butter and swirl or stir quickly to melt and emulsify the butter into the sauce, which will thicken slightly and make it nice and glossy.

5. Return cooked meat and any accumulated juices into skillet. Stir to coat steak bits in the pan sauce and serve immediately. Enjoy!

Nutrition Value

Calories: 269kcal| Carbohydrates: 1g| Protein: 23g| Fat: 17g|

62. Cast Iron Meatballs

Prep Time: 10 minutes Cook Time: 25 minutes

Total Time: 54 minutes Servings: 4

Ingredients

- 1 lb ground beef
- 1 egg
- 1/3 cup almond flour
- 1 tsp dried oregano
- 1/2 tsp crushed red pepper

- 1/2 tsp garlic powder
- 1/2 tsp black pepper
- 1 1/2 tsp salt
- 1 tbsp avocado oil
- Optional: 24oz jar of marinara sauce

Instructions

1. Preheat oven to 350F and add avocado oil to a 10″ cast iron skillet
2. In a large mixing, bowl combine ground beef, egg, almond flour, salt, pepper, garlic powder, oregano, and crushed red pepper
3. Mix until evenly combined and roll into 12 even balls – each ball will be a little over 2 tbsp worth
4. Heat oil in cast-iron skillet over medium heat
5. When oil is hot, add the meatballs to the pan to cook
6. Continue cooking for about 6 minutes rotating occasionally until meatballs are browned on all sides
7. Place the cast-iron skillet in the oven at 350F and bake for 12 minutes
8. Enjoy without sauce or add a jar of marinara directly to the skillet with the meatballs and warm on the stove at medium-low heat for 5 minutes

Nutrition Facts

Calories: 362kcal Total Fat: 13.1g| Carbohydrate 3.4g Protein 37.2g

63. Beef And Sweet Potato Skillet

Servings: 4 Prep Time: 10 minutes

Total Time: 30 minutes

Ingredients

- 2 tbsp. Gustare Vita olive oil
- 1 (1-lbs.) pkg. lean ground beef
- 2 large sweet potatoes, peeled and chopped, about 3 c.
- ½ c. red onion, chopped
- 1 tsp. garlic powder
- 1 tsp. ground cumin
- 1 tsp. salt
- ½ tsp. ground cinnamon
- 1 (15-oz.) can Hy-Vee diced tomatoes, undrained
- 1 c. fresh spinach, packed
- 1 lime, juiced
- Fresh cilantro, for garnish, if desired
- 1 avocado, peeled, pitted, and sliced

Instruction

1. Heat oil in large nonstick skillet over medium-high heat. Add potatoes; cook 5 to 7 minutes or until tender and lightly browned. Remove from skillet; set aside.
2. Add beef and onion to skillet; sprinkle with salt, cinnamon, garlic powder and pepper. Cook and stir 4 to 5 minutes or until beef is cooked through.
3. Add undrained tomatoes to skillet; simmer 2 minutes or until hot. Stir in cooked potatoes. Serve immediately

Nutrition facts

Calories: 364kcal Total Fat: 20g| | Carbohydrates: 33g| | Protein: 27g

64. Beef And Broccoli Recipe

Servings: 4 Servings Prep Time: 10 Minutes

Cook Time: 15 Minutes Total Time: 25 Minutes

Ingredients

- 1/2 cup soy sauce
- 2 tbsp brown sugar
- 1 tsp ground ginger
- 1/2 tsp red pepper flakes
- 1/2 cup beef broth
- 3 tbsp cornstarch, divided
- 2 tbsp cold water
- 1 tbsp minced garlic

- 3 tbsp olive oil, divided
- 1 lb flank steak, trimmed and thinly sliced
- 5 cups broccoli florets
- 1 cup onion wedges

Instructions

1. Mix soy sauce, brown sugar, ginger, pepper flakes, one Tbsp of cornstarch, and beef broth. Set it aside.
2. In a separate bowl, mix two Tbsp of cornstarch, water, and garlic. Add the sliced beef and stir to coat.
3. Heat two Tbsp of oil in a frying pan over medium-high heat and stir fry the coated beef for 3-4 minutes until cooked through. Remove the beef from the frying pan and set it aside.
4. Add the broccoli and onions to the frying pan and stir fry for 3-5 minutes, until tender.
5. Return the beef to the pan. Add the soy sauce mixture. Cook and stir for 3-5 minutes, until thickened.
6. Serve the beef and broccoli over rice.

Nutrition Information

Calories: 269kcal Total Fat: 16g| | Carbohydrates: 25g| Protein: 31g

65. Easy Ground Beef And Broccoli

Prep Time: 5 minutes Cook Time: 10 minutes

Servings: 4

Ingredients

- 1 cup rice
- 1/4 cup soy sauce or low sodium soy sauce
- 1 teaspoon ground ginger or 1 tablespoon fresh minced ginger
- 4 cloves fresh garlic minced
- 2 tsp.s red wine vinegar
- 1 teaspoon sesame oil
- 1 tsp. Sriracha sauce optional
- 1 tsp. garlic chili sauce optional - will make it saltier
- 1 Tbsp olive oil
- 1 lb ground beef
- 12 oz fresh broccoli florets or frozen
- 1 Tbsp sesame seeds

Instructions

1. Bring two cups of water to a boil. Add rice and then lower to a simmer and cover. Let cook for 15 - 20 minutes or according to package instructions.
2. In a small bowl, add soy sauce, ground ginger, garlic, red wine vinegar, sesame oil, sriracha, and garlic chili sauce and mix well.
3. In a large skillet, heat olive oil over medium-high heat and add ground beef. Cook for 3-5 minutes, crumbling as you cook. Then drain and discard the excess fat.
4. Add broccoli and then soy sauce mixture and then let simmer for about 5-7 minutes until broccoli is tender
5. Sprinkle with sesame seeds and serve over rice.

Nutrition

Calories: 554kcal | Carbohydrates: 46g | Protein: 27g | Fat: 29g |

66. Skillet Shredded Beef Nachos

Prep Time: 10 Minutes Cook Time: 10 Minutes

Total Time: 20 Minutes Servings: 4

Ingredients

- 1/2 a large bag of thick tortilla chips
- 2 cups shredded barbacoa beef
- 1 1/2 cups shredded Monterey Jack cheese, divided
- 1 cup shredded cheddar cheese
- ½ cup diced red onion
- ½ cup diced bell pepper
- 1 tomato, chopped
- 1 jalapeno, sliced

- Sour cream
- Chopped cilantro

Instructions

1. Preheat oven to 400 degrees.
2. In a large cast-iron skillet, layer 1/2 of the tortilla chips with 1/2 each of the cheeses, beef, onions, and peppers.
3. Repeat with the second layer of chips, cheese, beef, and veggies, reserving a half-cup of cheese for the top.
4. Place the nachos in the oven and bake for 7-10 minutes, or until cheese is melted.
5. Remove from the oven and top with tomatoes, chopped cilantro, sour cream, and sliced jalapenos, if desired.
6. Serve immediately.

Nutrition Information

Calories: 343 kcal Total Fat: 27g| Carbohydrates: 8g | Protein: 36g

67. Slow-Cooked Red Wine Beef Stew

Prep Time: 25 mins Cook Time: 2 hrs 30 mins

Total Time: 2 hrs 55 mins Servings 4

Ingredients

- Stew
- 3 pounds beef chuck roast
- 1 tablespoon kosher salt, or 1 ½ teaspoons table salt
- 3 Tbsp olive oil
- 2-3 shallots, finely chopped (1 cup)
- 3 Tbsp all-purpose flour
- 1 tablespoon tomato paste
- 4 whole garlic cloves, peeled
- ½ teaspoon freshly ground black pepper
- 1 ½ cups hearty dry red wine
- 1-2 cups beef or chicken broth
- 2 bay leaves and 4 sprigs each thyme and rosemary
- 1 pound carrots, peeled and sliced into 2-inch chunks
- 2 leeks, chopped
- 1 fennel bulb, stems, and tough outer layers trimmed, sliced into ½-inch wedges
- 2 stalks celery, chopped
- 1 Tbsp (15 ml) extra-virgin olive oil
- ¼ cup chopped fresh parsley
- ½ tsp. kosher salt

Instructions

1. Heat oven to 350 degrees F with the rack in the center.
2. Prep the beef: Trim the meat of excess fat and slice it into 3-inch chunks. Season evenly on all sides with 2 teaspoons salts.
3. Heat the oil in a large Dutch oven or heavy casserole over medium-high heat. Sear the beef in batches until browned. Remove to a platter.
4. Lower the heat to medium and add the shallot to the pot. Cook 5 minutes, stirring now and then, until softened. Return the beef to the pot and sprinkle with flour. Stir in the tomato paste, garlic, wine, 1 teaspoon salt, and pepper.
5. Bring to a simmer, then adds enough broth to just cover the beef. Toss in the herb bundle. Cover the pot with a sheet of parchment or foil, then top with the pot lid.
6. Place in the oven to braise for 2 ½-3 hours. The cooking liquid will be slightly reduced and the meat should fall apart when prodded with a fork.
7. Cook the vegetables
8. Put the carrots, leeks, fennel, and celery in a large skillet with ¼ cup water, 1 Tbsp extra-virgin olive oil, and 1/2 tsp. salt. Place over high heat until the water boils. Lower heat to a simmer. Cover the pan and cook until the vegetables are tender but still colorful about 10-12 minutes.
9. To serve, stir the vegetables into the stew. Taste for seasoning, adding more salt and pepper as desired. Sprinkle with the parsley.

Nutrition Facts

Calories: 269kcal Carbohydrates: 22g | Protein: 46g | Fat: 36g |

68. Classic French Beef Bourguignon

Prep Time: 40 minutes Cook Time: 3 hours

Total Time: 3 hours 40 minutes Servings: 6

Ingredients

- Vegetable oil
- 6 ounces bacon, sliced
- 2 lb beef chuck roast, cubed in 1 ½" pieces
- 1 large onion, sliced
- ¾ lb carrots, peeled & cut into 1" pieces
- 1 Tbsp garlic, minced
- 12 ounces frozen pearl onions
- 3 cups red wine
- 1 ½ cups beef broth
- 1 Tbsp tomato paste
- ½ teaspoon dried thyme
- ¾ lb mushrooms, sliced
- 3 Tbsp unsalted butter
- 3 tablespoon flour
- Salt
- Black pepper

Instructions

1. Preheat oven to 300F.
2. Place 3 Tbsp butter in a small bowl and let sit at room temperature. When soft add 3 Tbsp flour and mix.
3. Bring a LARGE ovenproof stock pot (a 6-quart dutch oven works perfectly) to medium-high heat and add a touch of vegetable oil to coat the pan lightly. When the oil is hot add the bacon. Cook ~ 4-6 minutes or until brown, strain, and place in a large bowl. Keep the fat in the pan and add the beef.
4. Generously salt and pepper the cubed beef. Sear beef on two sides for 3-5 minutes each or until brown. Place into the bowl with bacon. You may need to brown the beef in batches if the pan is not large enough. You want it to brown and not steam (which will happen if the pan is crowded).
5. Keep any fat in the pan (add more if needed) and add onions, mushrooms, ½ teaspoon sea salt, and ½ tsp. black pepper. Reduce heat, cook uncovered low ~ 10 minutes or until onions start to brown/caramelize. Add garlic and cook 1-2 minutes or until fragrant.
6. Add carrots, bacon, beef, and any juices back to the pan. Stir in tomato paste. Add frozen pearl onions, red wine, thyme, and enough beef broth to nearly cover the meat (you may not need all two cups).
7. Cover and bake in the oven for 2 hours or until beef & vegetables are tender.
8. Take the stew out of the oven, bring to a simmer, and stir in the flour/butter mixture.
9. Bring the stew back to a boil covered on the stovetop. Reduce heat and simmer uncovered ~15 minutes or until thickened.
10. Add sea salt to taste. Serve with toasted thick-cut country bread, egg noodles, or mashed potatoes.

Nutrition Facts

Calories: 364kcal Total Fat: 29.1g| Total Carbohydrate: 66.4gProtein: 44.2g

69. Cast Iron Pan-Seared Steak & Au Jus

Prep Time: 5 minutes Cook Time: 10 minutes

Total Time: 15 minutes Servings: 6

Ingredients

- 3 lbs. Thick cut ribeye steak, or your choice
- 1 tbsp olive oil
- 1 tbsp butter
- 1 tsp garlic powder
- 1 tsp italian seasoning
- 1 tsp paprika
- 1 cup onion chopped

- ½ c. Red cooking wine- omit if keto
- 2 cloves garlic minced
- 1 c. Beef broth
- ¼ c. Heavy whipping cream
- Salt and pepper to taste

Instructions

1. Heat 1 Tbsp of oil and 1 Tbsp of butter over medium-high heat in a large skillet.
2. Apply seasonings, salt, and pepper to taste to both sides of your ribeye steaks.
3. Once the skillet is hot, place the steak into it and cook for 3-4 minutes on each side. NOTE* TIME MAY VARY depending on the size of your steak. Use the touch method or thermometer to reach your desired temp.
4. Do not move the steak around. Sear the sides all of the way around the edge of the steak as well to render the fat.
5. Remove the steak from the skillet, wrap in foil to rest.
6. Add chopped onion to the pan juices. Cook for 2-3 minutes until the onions begin to soften and brown.
7. Add 2 cloves of minced garlic to the pan and stir, cooking for an additional minute. Add a shake of Italian Seasoning or Thyme.
8. Pour in ½ cup of red cooking wine, and scrape the bottom of the pan to deglaze it. Cook the wine down until it is reduced by at least half. Approximately 5 minutes of bubbling.
9. Mix in broth. Continue to cook it down until it begins to thicken.
10. Add in ¼ cup of heavy whipping cream. Stir and cook the pan gravy down until it has reached your desired consistency.
11. Slice the ribeye steak, and plate is served with a bed of greens and smothered in the pan gravy.

Nutrition Information

Calories: 350

70. Ground Beef Taco Meat

Prep Time: 5 mins Cook Time: 15 mins

Total Time: 20 mins Servings: 6

Ingredients

- 2 tsp. olive oil
- ½ yellow onion (diced)
- 1 pound lean ground beef
- 2 tsp. chili powder
- ¼ teaspoon garlic powder
- ½ tsp. dried oregano
- ¼ tsp. paprika
- ½ tsp. dried cumin
- ½ tsp. crushed red pepper (optional)
- Salt and pepper (to taste)
- ¼ tsp. cornstarch (optional)
- 1 cup tomato sauce

Instructions

1. Heat a large skillet over medium-high heat. Add the oil and diced onion and sauté for 4-5 minutes, or until the onions are soft. Stir often to prevent burning and reduce heat to medium if needed.
2. Add the ground beef to the skillet. Use a large wooden spoon or spatula to break the beef into smaller and smaller bits and pieces. Fully cook your ground beef before draining approximately 3/4 of the liquid and fat from the skillet.
3. Return the skillet to medium-high heat. Add the spices and tomato sauce to the beef and mix well to combine. Continue to cook for an additional 5 minutes or so, stirring often.
4. Serve with all your favorite taco dinners! Enjoy!

Nutritional Information

Calories: 201kcal | Carbohydrates: 5g | Protein: 25g | Fat: 8g |

71. Chimichurri Ground Beef And Rice Recipe

Prep Time: 5 minutes Cook Time: 25 minutes

Total Time: 30 minutes Servings: 3

Ingredients

Chimichurri Sauce:

- 1/4 cup extra virgin olive oil
- 2 TBSP red wine vinegar
- 1/2 tsp dried oregano
- 1/4 tsp cumin
- 1/4 tsp salt
- 1 clove garlic
- 1/2 cup fresh parsley
- 1/2 cup fresh cilantro
- 1 tsp red pepper flakes, optional

Ground Beef And Rice Skillet

- 1 lb ground beef
- 1 tbsp olive oil
- 1 yellow onion
- 1 orange pepper
- 1 cup rice
- 1.5 cups water
- 1 cup corn
- 2 cup cherry tomatoes, halved

Instructions

1. In a food processor, blend the olive oil, red wine vinegar, oregano, cumin, salt, garlic, parsley, and cilantro (and red pepper flakes, if desired) until smooth. Set aside.
2. In a large cast-iron skillet, heat 1 TBSP olive oil over medium-high heat.
3. Cook the ground beef, stirring occasionally, for 5-8 minutes, or until no longer pink.
4. Add in the onion and pepper and continue cooking an additional 5 minutes, stirring occasionally, until the peppers and onions are starting to soften.
5. Add in the rice and water, cover with a lid and allow simmering for 15 minutes.
6. Remove the lid, stir in the corn and cherry tomatoes, and then replace the lid.
7. Turn off the heat and allow to sit for an additional 10 minutes.
8. Fluff with a fork and serve with the chimichurri sauce.

Nutrition Information

Calories: 269kcal Total Fat: 38gCarbohydrates: 28g| | Protein: 35g

72. Cast Iron Skillet Steak

Prep Time: 5 minutes Cook Time: 12 minutes

Servings: 2

Ingredients

- 16 ounces ribeye steak
- 4 Tbsp unsalted butter
- 5 garlic cloves
- 4 sprigs of fresh rosemary
- Kosher salt
- Freshly ground pepper

Instructions

1. About one hour before cooking, remove the ribeye from the fridge and pat dry with paper towels. Season generously with salt and pepper and allow to come to room temperature.
2. Place a deep cast-iron skillet over medium-high heat.
3. Once the skillet is hot, pat the steak dry one more time - just removing any moisture, not the seasoning. Then place the steak in the hot pan.
4. After about 3-4 minutes, a nice crust should form on the steak, flip it over for another 3-4 minutes and check

the temperature. If steak has not reached the desired temperature, keep flipping it over and checking the temperature every 2 minutes or so. Total cook time will depend on the thickness of the steak.

5. Just before steak reaches the desired temperature, add butter, garlic, and rosemary to the pan. Let rosemary and garlic sizzle in the butter for a bit. Then carefully tip the pan toward you so the butter pools, and spoon it over the steak a few times.

6. Remove the steak from the hot pan and allow to rest for 5 minutes before slicing and serving.

Nutrition Value

Calories: 684kcal | Carbohydrates: 3g | Protein: 46g | Fat: 55g

73. Dutch Oven Pot Roast With Carrots And Potatoes

Cook Time: 3 hours 15 minutes Total Time: 3 hours 25 minutes Servings: 6 people

Ingredients

- 2 Tbsp vegetable or olive oil
- 1/2 red onion sliced
- 2-pound chuck roast
- 1 teaspoon salt
- 1/2 teaspoon black pepper
- 4 cups beef broth
- 3 large russet potatoes peeled and sliced into 1-inch wedges
- 5 large carrots peeled and sliced into 1-inch thick pieces

Instructions

1. Preheat the oven to 375.

2. Put your dutch oven on the stove and heat it over high heat for about 5 minutes to sear the meat. (Please watch your pot and monitor the heat. Your pot may only need 3 minutes or 4. Y'all stop trying to burn your houses down because I said 5 minutes) Add the oil and season the meat with salt and pepper on both sides. Add it to the pan. It should sizzle immediately.

3. Reduce the heat to medium-high, and let the meat sear on one side for 5 minutes, then flip. Add the onions and cook 5 minutes more.

4. Add the beef broth to the pot--it should come about halfway up the side of the meat.

5. Cover and bake an hour and a half, then check the liquid in the pot. Add a cup or so of extra water if needed.

6. Reduce the heat to 350 and bake an additional hour, and then add the carrots and potatoes. Bake covered 45 minutes longer or until the meat is tender and the potatoes and carrots are soft.

Nutrition Value

Calories: 498kcal | Carbohydrates: 40g | Protein: 35g | Fat: 23g |

74. One Skillet Coffee-Rubbed Steak And Potatoes

Servings: 4 servings Prep Time: 20 minutes

Cook Time: 30 minutes Total Time: 50 minutes

Ingredients

- 1 pound skirt steak, cut into four equal pieces
- 1/4 cup fresco spice blends coffee steak rub
- 5 Tbsp avocado oil, divided
- 4 Tbsp butter or ghee, divided
- 1 pound yukon gold potatoes, cut into 1/2" pieces
- 4 cloves garlic, finely minced
- 1 pound brussels sprouts, trimmed and quartered
- 1 tablespoon fresh thyme, chopped
- 1 Tbsp rosemary, chopped
- Salt and pepper, to taste

Instructions

1. Place the skirt steak sections onto a large cutting board.

2. Cover both sides of the steak liberally with the Fresco Spice Blends Coffee Steak Rub. Cover loosely, and set aside on the counter to come up to room temperature.

3. In a 10" or larger cast iron skillet, heat 2 Tbsp of avocado oil and 2 Tbsp butter or ghee over high heat.

4. Add in the potatoes, stir to coat with the fats, and then cook until the undersides have a nice, crispy sear on them—about 3 minutes. Stir and reduce heat to medium. Cook, stirring occasionally until most of the potatoes are golden brown, and the texture is just before fork-tender (you want a little resistance when you push the fork in), about 10 minutes.

5. Push the potatoes to one side of the skillet, then add one Tbsp of avocado oil to the empty side of the skillet. Add in the garlic in the space, and sauté until just softened and fragrant, about a minute.

6. Add the Brussels sprouts and spread to fill the space, and cook until the bottom side of the sprouts begins to caramelize and turn brown, about 5 minutes.

7. Mix up the potatoes and Brussels sprouts in the skillet and continue to cook, stirring occasionally, until both the potatoes and Brussels sprouts are fork tender, about 5 more minutes.

8. Add in the thyme and rosemary, season with salt and pepper, then transfer to a plate and keep warm.

9. Return the skillet to high heat, and then add in the remaining avocado oil and butter or ghee. If using a 10" skillet, add two pieces of the skirt steak at a time.

10. Cook until the underside has a nice sear, about 2 minutes. Flip the meat and cook an additional minute for a rare steak, or an additional 2-3 minutes for a well-done steak.

11. Remove steak and let rest on a cutting board, and then repeat with remaining steak pieces. If using a 12" or larger skillet, you should be able to fit all four pieces in the skillet at once.

12. Allow the steak to rest for 10 minutes, then slice across the grain into long, thin strips. Serve immediately with Brussels sprouts and potatoes.

Nutrition Information

Calories: 369kcal Total Fat: 59g Carbohydrates: 37g| Protein: 49g

75. Ribeye Steaks With Red Wine Sauce

Prep Time: 15 mins Cook Time: 40 mins

Total Time: 55 mins Servings: 2 servings

Ingredients

- 2 large ribeye steaks, 1½ to 2-inches thick
- Kosher salt, as needed for seasoning
- Black pepper, as needed for seasoning
- 1 tablespoon vegetable oil
- 2 Tbsp unsalted butter, divided
- 1 Tbsp minced garlic
- ¼ cup minced shallots
- 1 cup red wine, zinfandel
- 1 Tbsp balsamic vinegar
- 1 sprig rosemary, plus more for garnish
- 2 sprigs thyme, plus more for garnish
- 1 cup beef stock
- ¼ cup parsley leaves, roughly chopped

Instructions

1. Line a sheet pan with foil and place a wire rack on top, set aside.

2. Adjust oven rack to the center position and preheat to 275°f

3. Place a large 12-inch cast-iron skillet in the oven to warm.

4. Dry the steaks with a paper towel to remove excess surface moisture and transfer them to the wire rack. Generously season the meat with salt and ground black pepper on both sides.

5. Place steaks in the oven and cook for about 15 to 25 minutes, depending on the thickness.

6. Remove the steaks from the oven and set them aside.

7. Remove the cast iron pan from the oven and transfer it to the stovetop.

8. Heat pan over high heat and add the oil.

9. Once the oil is very hot and just beginning to smoke, carefully add the steaks to the pan.

10. Sear the first side until a deep brown crust is formed, about 2 minutes.

11. Carefully flip the steaks over and sear for about 1 ½ to 2 minutes.

12. Use tongs to turn the steaks on their sides to cook and render the remaining fat, about 2 minutes total.

13. Add one Tbsp of the butter to the pan, melt and use a spoon to briefly baste the tops of the steaks.

14. Transfer steaks to a clean plate and allow to rest at room temperature for 10 minutes.

15. For the red wine sauce, reserve 1 Tbsp of the steak drippings in the cast iron pan and heat over medium.

16. Once the drippings are warm add the garlic and shallots, saute and stir frequently until tender, about 1 minute.

17. Add red wine, balsamic vinegar, rosemary sprig, and thyme sprigs, bring mixture to a rapid simmer over high heat.

18. Allow wine mixture to reduce until thickened, about ¼ a cup, 3 to 5 minutes.

19. Add in beef stock, and rapidly simmer over high heat until the sauce is reduced and thickened to about ½ cup, about 4 to 5 minutes.

20. Remove rosemary and thyme, discard.

21. Turn off heat and whisk in 1 Tbsp of butter.

22. Taste the red wine sauce and season with more salt and pepper as desired.

23. Garnish steaks with chopped thyme, rosemary, and parsley a few minutes before serving.

Nutrition Facts

Calories: 269kcal Fat: 68g | Carbohydrates: 6g| Protein: 42g

FISH AND SEAFOOD

76. Cast Iron Halibut Dinner With Couscous

Prep Time: 10 Mins Cook Time: 20 Mins

Servings: 4

Ingredients

Couscous

- 1 cup pearl couscous
- 1 tsp freshly chopped dill
- 1 tbsp olive oil extra virgin
- 1.25 cups water
- 1 tbsp freshly squeezed lemon juice
- Pinch salt to taste

Halibut

- 4 halibut fillets standard is 6 ozs but you can go up to 8 ozs if desired
- 10-12 cherry tomatoes
- 2 tbsp olive oil extra virgin
- 1 tsp coarse Mediterranean sea salt useless if trying to keep sodium low
- 1 tbsp fresh chopped dill add extra for garnish as needed
- 1 lemon
- 0.5 tsp white pepper

Instructions

Couscous

1. Get couscous started first and once it is cooking, I sear the halibut so both finish cooking almost simultaneously.
2. Add 1 tbsp of olive oil in a small to a medium pot. Set heat to medium. Then add a cup of couscous, toast slightly using a wooden spoon. This gives couscous a nutty flavor.
3. Add 1.25 cups of water (pre-heat water if you can in an electric kettle). Then add a pinch of salt, dill, and lemon juice. Mix it once. Once the water boils, cover with a lid and lower heat to simmer. Couscous should be done in about 10 minutes. Turn heat off! Set pot aside. When ready to serve fluff up with a fork, then garnish with fresh dill and lemon slices.
4. Since couscous cooks so fast, I don't cook in huge quantities to avoid leftovers. It always tastes better when cooked fresh!

Halibut

1. Use fresh halibut or thawed halibut fillets. Pat dry fillets with a paper towel. Then season with coarse Mediterranean salt, white pepper, fresh dill on both sides. Sprinkle fresh lemon juice over fillets.
2. Place cast-iron skillet on the stovetop, medium heat until skillet is hot. Add olive oil to the skillet.
3. Place halibut fillets carefully on the cast iron skillet. Don't move them around or try to flip them. You'll flip them only once after 3-4 minutes. Usually fish becomes white from the bottom up. Flip carefully, it helps to use a fish spatula. Let cook on the other side as well for the same amount of time. Towards the last 2 minutes add the cherry tomatoes around the skillet. You want them to sear lightly but not overcook. Don't stir the tomatoes!
4. Garnish with fresh dill and lemon slices. I also sprinkle fresh lemon juice over fish right before serving. It's best to serve right away for the best flavor. Enjoy

Nutrition Value

Calories: 425kcal| Carbohydrates: 38g| Protein: 38g| Fat: 13g|

77. Grilled Lingcod

Cook Time: 10 minutes Total Time: 10 minutes

Servings: 4 servings

Ingredients

- 2 lbs Lingcod
- 1 tbsp Olive Oil
- 2 tbsp Butter

Instructions

1. Heat the grill to 375 degrees on direct heat. Place the cast iron flat top griddle on the grate.
2. The cast iron is ready when you can add a drop of water to the surface and it immediately started sizzling.
3. Add the butter and olive oil to the cast iron and use a spatula to cover the surface.

4. Add the lingcod fillets and let them cook for 3 – 4 minutes.
5. They are ready to turn over if they are easy to lift off the cast iron with a spatula. That shows that they have been properly seared.
6. Turn them over and cook the other side for 3 – 4 minutes.
7. Remove from the grill and serve with slices of lemon.

Nutrition Value

Calories: 268kcal | Carbohydrates: 1g | Protein: 40g | Fat: 11g |

78. Southern Fried Cat Fish

Prep Time: 10 mins Cook Time: 30 mins

Total Time: 40 mins Servings: 4

Ingredients

- 1 1/2 cup cornmeal
- 1 Tbsp Granulated garlic
- 1 Tsp. onion powder
- 1/2 -1 tsp.s cayenne pepper
- 1 teaspoon white or black pepper
- 2 tsp.s salt adjust to taste
- 1 1/2 cup buttermilk
- 4 6-ounce catfish fillets (cut in small chunks)

Spicy Tartar Sauce

- 1 cup mayonnaise
- 1 tablespoon finely diced onion
- 1/2-1 teaspoon mustard sauce
- 3 Tbsp hot pepper relish
- 1 Tbsp granulated garlic
- Dash hot sauce
- Salt and pepper to taste

Instructions

1. Preheat a deep-fryer to 375 degrees F or In a large, saucepan pour vegetable oil - halfway.
2. In a large bowl mix together, cornmeal, garlic, onion powder, cayenne, salt, and pepper.
3. If fish fillet too large cut into bite-sized pieces.
4. Dip each strip in buttermilk and lightly deep into the remaining cornmeal.
5. Deep fry the fish in the fryer or saucepan a few pieces at a time, moving them around so they don't stick. Fry until brown and crispy, about 3 to 4 minutes or more depending on the size. These big chunks took about 6 minutes per side.
6. Remove from the fryer with a slotted spoon place on a cookie rack to ensure crispness. Repeat with the remaining fillets and season the fish with lemon juice. Serve with spicy tartar sauce

Spicy Tartar Sauce

1. In a serving bowl combine mayonnaise, garlic, hot pepper relish, onions, mustards, dash hot sauce, salt, and pepper.
2. Cover with plastic wrap and let the flavors mellow in the refrigerator for at least 1 hour before serving.

Nutrition Information

Calories: 146kcal| Carbohydrates: 18g| Protein: 11g| Fat: 3g|

79. Cast Iron Salmon

Prep Time: 5 mins Cook Time: 15 mins

Total Time: 20 mins Servings: 4 people

Ingredients

- 16 ounces farm-raised salmon, cut into 4 ounce filets
- 1 teaspoon ghee, or coconut or avocado oil
- 1 teaspoon kosher salt, I like this one
- 1/2 teaspoon black pepper

Instructions

1. Pre-heat oven to 450 Fahrenheit and place 12-inch cast-iron skillet in the oven to heat up.
2. Use a paper towel to pat both sides of salmon dry. If the skin is wet, it won't get crispy.
3. Patting salmon with a paper towel
4. Season the salmon skin with kosher salt.
5. Sprinkling salt on salmon skin
6. Carefully, remove the hot pan from the oven and melt ghee in the pan.
7. Ghee melting in a hot pan
8. Add salmon, skin side down, to the pan. You want to hear a sizzling sear when it hits the pan. Season top of

salmon with a little more salt and black pepper and place in the oven for about 15 minutes.
9. Seasoning salmon in cast iron skillet
10. Once the salmon is opaque and flaky and opaque, it's ready to serve. I usually just stick a fork in and twist to make sure my salmon is done.
11. Flaking off the salmon with a fork
12. Serve and enjoy!

Nutrition Value

| Calories: 173kcal | Carbohydrates: 1g | Protein: 23g | Fat: 8g |

80. Cast Iron Grilled Tilapia

Prep Time: 10 mins Cook Time: 15 mins

Servings: 4

Ingredients

- 1 tbsp olive oil
- 1 onion sliced thin
- 2 tilapia filets
- ½ tsp paprika
- ½ tsp garlic powder
- ¼ tsp dried oregano
- 3 tbsp butter divided

Instructions

Prep Your Grill For Cooking:

1. Arrange heated coals in an even layer and nestle a 10-inch cast-iron skillet directly over the coals. Allow the cast iron to heat up.
2. When the skillet has heated, add the olive oil and, using a heat-resistant glove and a long spatula, swirl to coat.
3. Lay the onion in the skillet and cover the grill. Cook until tender 5 to 7 minutes, checking occasionally and stirring.
4. Meanwhile, pat the tilapia dry.
5. In a small bowl, mix the paprika, garlic powder, and oregano.
6. Sprinkle liberally over the tilapia filets on both sides.
7. Add one Tbsp of butter to the skillet and slide the onions to the outer edges.
8. Lay the tilapia directly into the skillet.
9. Top each fillet with a tablespoon of butter.
10. Cover the lid and allow the tilapia to cook through, 5 to 7 minutes until it flakes easily with a fork.
11. With heat-resistant gloves, remove the skillet from the fire and transfer it to a serving area.
12. If making more than 2 filets, leave the skillet on the fire, and transfer the onions and tilapia to a serving dish with a spatula and repeat as needed for quantity.

Nutrition Facts

Calories: 269kcal Fat: 14g| Carbohydrates: 3g| Protein: 18g|

81. Classic Seafood Stew

Prep Time: 10 Minutes Cook Time: 1 Hour

Servings: 4

Ingredients

- 2 tbsp olive oil
- 2 small shallots minced
- 2 stalks celery minced
- 3 cloves garlic minced
- 1/2 tsp red pepper flakes
- 1 cup cherry tomatoes
- 8 oz. clam juice
- 3 cups chicken broth
- 1 cup chardonnay
- 1 tsp kosher salt
- 1/2 tsp black pepper
- 2 bay leaves
- 1 lb clams
- 1 lb shrimp
- 1/2 lb scallops
- 2 tbs butter
- 2 tbs flour

Instructions

1. Heat grill to medium. Place a large cast-iron pot on the grill. Heat the olive oil. Sauté the shallots, celery, garlic, and red pepper flakes, until tender. Add the tomatoes and sauté for 3 minutes.

2. Add the clam juice, chicken broth, wine, salt, pepper, and bay leaves. Top with a lid, close the grill, and simmer for 30 minutes.
3. Remove the lid. Add the clams. Close the grill, and cook for 10 minutes. Add the scallops and shrimp and grill for 5 minutes.
4. Combine the butter and flour in a small bowl, and roll into 3 balls. Drop the balls into the pot and cook, stirring occasionally for 5 minutes.
5. Serve with grilled bread.

Nutrition Value

Calories: 394kcal| Carbohydrates: 16g| Protein: 34g| Fat: 15g|

82. Skillet Blackened Tilapia

Prep Time: 15 minutes Cook Time: 10 minutes

Total Time: 25 minutes Servings: 4 servings

Ingredients

- 24 oz. tilapia – about four large filets
- 3 Tbsp canola oil
- For the blackened seasoning:
- 1 Tbsp paprika
- 1 Tbsp brown sugar
- 1 teaspoon garlic powder
- 1 teaspoon onion powder
- 1 teaspoon cumin
- 1/2 tsp. red pepper flakes
- 1 teaspoon cayenne pepper
- 1 tsp. kosher salt
- freshly ground black pepper – to taste

Instructions

1. Prepare the blackened seasoning by combining all ingredients.
2. Take the tilapia and pat dry with a paper towel. Layout on pan or plate, and spread blackened seasoning on both sides of fish. Massage seasoning into fish with hands.
3. Heat skillet to medium-high heat. Add half of the oil to the pan and when heated, add two pieces of tilapia.
4. Cook for 2-3 minutes, and flip, cooking another 2-3 minutes. If you have large, thick pieces of fish, you may need to cook longer. The fish is done when it flakes easily with a fork.
5. Repeat with the remaining two pieces of fish.
6. Serve blackened tilapia over rice and vegetables if desired.

Nutrition Value

Calories: 275kcal | Carbohydrates: 3g | Protein: 35g | Fat: 14g |

83. Cast Iron Skillet Cod With Garlic Butter

Prep Time: 10 Minutes Cook Time: 10 Minutes

Total Time: 20 Minutes Servings: 4

Ingredients

For The Garlic Butter:

- 2 Tbsp unsalted butter (softened)
- 2 tsp chopped parsley
- 1/2 tsp minced garlic
- 1 tsp minced onion
- 1/4 tsp Dijon mustard
- 1/2 Tbsp all-purpose flour
- 1/2 Tbsp lemon juice
- Salt to taste
- Black pepper to taste

For The Cod:

- 1 Tbsp cooking oil
- 2 skinless cod fillets (7 oz each)
- Lemon wedges for garnish

Instructions

1. Preheat the oven to 450 degrees F (230 C).
2. In a small bowl, stir together the softened butter, parsley, minced garlic, minced onion, Dijon mustard, flour, lemon juice, salt, and pepper. Set aside.
3. Heat the oil in a cast-iron skillet over medium-high heat. Click for a cast-iron skillet.
4. Season the cod fillets with salt and pepper and cook for 4 minutes.
5. Turn the cod fillets over and cook for 1 minute.
6. Spoon 1/2 Tbsp each of the butter mixture over the top of the fish fillets. The remaining butter will be used later.

7. Transfer the cast iron skillet to the oven and bake for 2 – 4 minutes or until fish is just cooked through and opaque in the center.
8. Add any remaining butter to the pan, and let melt, stirring with juices in the pan.
9. Spoon the pan butter over the fish and garnish with the lemon wedges, if desired. Serve immediately.

Nutrition Information

Calories: 274 kcal Total Fat: 19g | Carbohydrates: 7g| Protein: 8g

84. Pan-Seared Fish Fillet

Prep Time: 10 mins Cook Time: 5 mins

Total Time: 15 mins Servings: 4

Ingredients

- 1 (8 oz) fish fillets, such as cod, snapper, sea bass, or salmon, with the skin on
- Ghee or grapeseed oil
- 1 to 2 Tbsp ghee or unsalted butter (optional)
- 1/2 lemon
- Sea salt and freshly ground black pepper

Instructions

1. Set a heavy cast iron or stainless steel skillet over medium-high heat until very hot but not smoking, about 3 minutes.
2. While the skillet is heating, wash the fillet, then pat it dry with paper towels. The drying part is critical, otherwise, the skin won't get crisp. Season both sides of the fish fillet with salt and black pepper.
3. When the skillet is hot, carefully add just enough ghee or oil to evenly coat the skillet.
4. Wait for a few seconds for the oil to heat and then quickly add the fish, skin side down. The fillet will contract and curve upwards. When this happens, take a flexible spatula and press the entire fillet gently back down and hold for a few seconds to ensure even cooking and crisp skin all over.
5. Let the fish cook without messing with it too much until you can see a golden brown color on the edge of the skin and the edges of the fish flesh become opaque, 3 to 4 minutes.
6. Carefully and gently use a spatula to lift the fillet and flip it over. Add the butter, if using, and baste the fish until cooked through, 2 to 3 minutes longer.
7. Gently transfer the fish to a plate and serve with a squeeze of lemon.

Nutritional Value

Calories: 324 kcal Carbohydrates: 3g| Protein: 46g| Fat: 19g|

85. Skillet Broiled Cod

Total Time: 30 minutes

Ingredients

- 1 lb. Cod filet thawed, patted dry
- 1 tbsp extra virgin olive oil
- Salt and pepper
- Old bay seasoning
- 1 cup corn
- 3-4 mini bell peppers sliced
- Cilantro and lime optional

Instructions

1. Preheat oven to low broil.
2. Sprinkle surface of cod filet with salt, pepper, and Old Bay seasoning.
3. Place in a skillet or on a pan; lay corn and bell peppers around it and drizzle with olive oil.
4. Place skillet in the center of top oven rack; broil (5-10 minutes) until fish becomes opaque and flakey when touched with a utensil; remove, allow to cool slightly; serve warm. (broil time depends on filet thickness)

Nutrition

Calories: 334cal | Carbohydrates: 18g | Protein: 43g | Fat: 9g

86. Blackened Fish

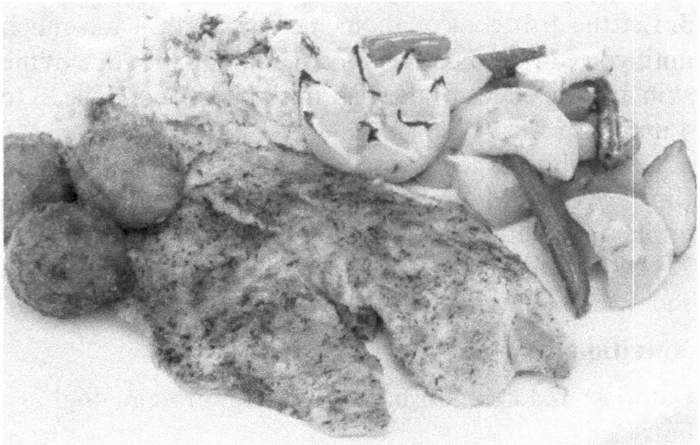

Prep Time: 5 Minutes Cook Time: 6 Minutes

Total Time: 11 Minutes Servings: 4

Ingredients

- 1 lb fish fillets (3-4 filets)
- 2 tbsp butter
- Salt and black pepper to taste
- 1 tsp garlic powder
- 1 tsp onion powder
- 1 tsp paprika
- 1 tsp Italian seasoning
- 1 tsp Old Bay seasoning
- 1/4 tsp cayenne pepper or up to 1/2 tsp to taste (optional)

Instructions

1. Combine the garlic powder, onion powder, paprika, Italian seasoning, Old Bay, and cayenne pepper (optional) and mix.
2. Lay the fish fillets flat and sprinkle seasonings on the first side, lightly pat them in, and then sprinkle the remaining seasoning on the backside and pat in. This can sit in the refrigerator for up to an hour seasoned.
3. Heat a large cast-iron skillet over high heat for 2-3 minutes, then reduce to medium-high and add the butter.
4. Once the butter is melted and starting to brown, but not smoke, season the fish with salt and pepper to taste, then put it flat in the skillet. Do not crowd the skillet. Cook the fish in batches if necessary.
5. Let the fish cook for 2-3 minutes on the first side without moving or checking it, then flip and cook for 2-3 minutes on the other side, or until it reaches the desired doneness, or about 145°F. Cooking time will vary depending on the size and thickness of your fish filets.
6. Remove the fish from the skillet (to prevent it from continuing to cook) and serve warm with fresh parsley or lemon juice if desired.

Nutrition Information

Calories: 274 kcal Carbohydrates: 2g| Protein: 24g| Fat: 7g|

87. Easy, Pan Seared Cast Iron Salmon

Prep Time: 5 Minutes Cook Time: 8 Minutes

Total Time: 28 Minutes Servings: 4

Ingredients

- 2-3 salmon fillets (skin-on, 6-8oz each)
- 1-2 Tbsp olive
- 1 tablespoon seafood
- Salt and pepper to taste
- 1/2 lemon

Instructions

1. If the salmon has been refrigerated, allow it to come to room temperature for 15 minutes and dry the salmon completely using paper towels. If the salmon is added to the skillet cold, it is more likely to stick to the skillet.
2. Rub olive oil onto both sides of the fish. Season both sides of the fish with seafood seasoning, salt, and pepper.
3. Place a cast-iron grill pan or cast-iron skillet on medium-high heat. I like to use a cast-iron grill pan, but any pan will work.
4. Spray or drizzle the skillet with olive oil. Be sure the skillet is nicely coated. This will prevent the salmon from sticking to the pan.
5. When the pan is hot, add the salmon to the pan with the skin side up. I like to add lemon halves lemon to the pan, too. This will add a ton of flavor to the lemon. (See recipe video)
6. Allow the salmon to cook for 4 minutes. Do not move the salmon after you have placed it in the skillet.
7. Monitor the sides of the salmon to determine the perfect time to flip. When the color of the side of the salmon has lightened about 3/4ths of the way up, it's time to flip. This usually only takes 3-4 minutes.
8. Flip the salmon. I find a silicone spatula works best. Remove the lemon and set it aside.
9. Cook skin side down for 4 minutes.
10. Remove the salmon from the pan. Serve with lemon juice from the lemon.

Nutrition Value

Calories: 249kcal | Carbohydrates: 2g | Protein: 34g | Fat: 13g

88. Skillet Salmon With Spring Ragout

Prep Time: 15 minutes Cook Time: 15 minutes

Servings: 2

Ingredients

- 14 1/2 ounce White Beans canned, drained, and rinsed
- 4 Tablespoon olive oil divided
- 1 cup carrots cleaned and diced
- 1 cup celery diced
- 1/4 cup shallot diced
- 1 clove garlic diced
- 1/2 teaspoon dried thyme
- 1/2 tsp. dried rosemary
- 3/4 pound salmon fillet
- Salt and pepper to taste

Instructions

1. Using a colander, drain and rinse the beans.
2. Chop the carrots, celery, and shallot. Chop the garlic and set it aside separately from the other vegetables.
3. Heat a cast-iron skillet over medium-high heat. Add 2 Tbsp of the oil. Once the oil is shimmering, add the carrots, celery, and shallot. Add the thyme and rosemary.
4. Cook, stirring often until the vegetables are starting to soften and are slightly toasted. Add in garlic and beans. Cook just until garlic is fragrant and beans are heated through. Using a spatula, remove vegetables from the pan to a plate. Cover to keep warm.
5. Wipe out the cast iron skillet with a paper towel and add the remaining two Tbsp of oil. Heat should be at medium to medium-high. Depending on your burner power.
6. When oil is hot, add the salmon skin side down. Salt and pepper to taste and add a squeeze of lemon if you'd like. Cook for 3 – 4 minutes, or until skin is crispy and salmon appears to be cooked about halfway through.
7. With a metal spatula, turn the salmon to cook on the flesh side. Cook for 2 – 3 minutes or until salmon appears to be done. Press on salmon. If it is starting to flake (flesh spreads apart), salmon is cooked.
8. To serve divide the salmon between two plates. Surround with the Spring Vegetable Bean Ragout. Serve immediately.

Nutrition Value

Calories: 803kcal | Carbohydrates: 58g | Protein: 55g | Fat: 40g |

89. Spicy Sweet Cast Iron Catfish

Prep Time: 5 Minutes Cook Time: 7 Minutes

Total Time: 12 Minutes Servings: 4

Ingredients

- 2-4 catfish filets
- 2 Tbsp canola oil
- Spicy Sweet Rub
- 1 Tbsp smoked paprika
- 1 tablespoon dark brown sugar
- 2 teaspoons dried oregano
- 1 teaspoon garlic powder
- 1 tsp. cumin
- 1/2 teaspoon salt
- 1/4 teaspoon cayenne pepper

Instructions

1. Preheat a cast-iron skillet with the canola oil on the grill, with the lid closed, to medium-high heat.
2. Mix spices together in a shallow dish. Rinse and pat dry catfish filets. Dredge the filets in the rub mixture, shaking off any excess.

3. Cook the fillets on one side for 3 minutes in the hot cast iron skillet with the grill lid closed. Flip and cook the other side another 3-4 minutes, or until the fish flakes easily.
4. Cook Mann's Bacon Maple Nourish Bowl according to package

Nutrition Information

Calories: 274 kcal Fat: 0.6g| Carbohydrates: 5.2g| Fiber: 1.1g| Protein: 27.6g

90. Healthy Codfish Skillet

Prep Time: 5 Mins Cook Time: 15 Mins

Total Time: 20 Mins Servings: 4

Ingredients

- 2 lbs. Fresh cod fillets
- 3 tbsp. Extra virgin olive oil
- 2 oz. Water
- 3 garlic cloves cut into thick slices
- 10 pitted black olives cut in half
- 1 medium tomato cut into bite-sized pieces
- 6 lemon slices
- Small bunch of fresh cilantro
- Salt and pepper to taste

Instructions

1. Place the cod fillets into a large skillet in a single layer. Season them with salt and pepper to taste.
2. Add the water and pour the olive oil over the fish.
3. Add the rest of the ingredients on top.
4. Cover with a lid, and cook on medium heat for 12-15 minutes, until the fish is cooked through and almost no liquid remains.
5. Remove the wilted cilantro and discard. Garnish with the freshly chopped cilantro, if desired.

Nutrition Value

Calories: 304kcal| Carbohydrates: 1g Protein: 40g| Fat: 14g|

91. Fish and Shrimp Pasta Skillet

Servings: 6 servings Prep Time: 10 minutes

Total Time: 30 minutes Servings: 4

Ingredients

- 3 c. penne rigate pasta
- 1 tbsp. unsalted butter
- 3 tbsp. plain panko bread crumbs
- ½ lbs. peel and deveined shrimp
- 1 lb. fresh cod, or tilapia fillets, cut into 3/4-inch cubes
- ½ tsp. kosher salt
- ½ tsp. lemon pepper seasoning
- 1 tbsp. canola oil
- 1 (12.5-oz.) jar Alfredo sauce
- ½ c. shredded Parmesan cheese
- ½ c. tomato, chopped
- Fresh Italian parsley, chopped
- Lemon slices, for serving

Instructions

1. Cook pasta according to package directions; drain, reserving 1/2 cup pasta water.
2. Keep pasta warm. Melt butter in a large deep skillet over medium heat. Stir in panko.
3. Cook and stir until panko is toasted; remove from skillet and set aside.
4. Peel shrimp; discard tails. Pat shrimp and cod dry.
5. Season with salt and lemon pepper.
6. Heat oil in the same skillet over medium-high heat.
7. Cook and stir shrimp and cod for 2 to 4 minutes or until shrimp are opaque and fish easily flakes with a fork (145 degrees).

8. Stir in hot pasta, Alfredo sauce, Parmesan cheese, and tomato; heat through. Add pasta water to thin sauce, if necessary.
9. Sprinkle with parsley and panko mixture. Serve with lemon slices.

Nutrition facts

Calories: 287 kcal Total Fat: 17g| Total Carbohydrates: 36g| Protein: 27g

92. Lobster Bisque

Prep Time: 20 Mins Cook Time: 30 Mins

Total Time: 50 Mins Servings: 4

Ingredients

- 2 Tbsp olive oil
- 2 Tbsp butter
- 1 yellow onion medium, diced small
- 2 ribs of celery diced small
- 1 carrot peeled and diced small
- 2 Tbsp tomato paste
- 3 cloves of garlic minced
- 1/2 teaspoon salt
- 1/8 tsp. white pepper Add up to 1/4 tsp.
- 1/8 tsp. cayenne Add up to 1/4 teaspoon
- 3 Tbsp flour
- 1/2 cup dry white wine
- 1 Tbsp Worcestershire sauce
- 1 box fish stock 32 ounces
- 1 bay leaf
- 3 sprigs of fresh thyme 1/2 teaspoon if using dried
- 1/2 cup heavy cream
- 1/2 pound cooked lobster meat approximately all the meat from two 1-1/2 pound lobsters
- Lemon zest optional

Instructions

1. Add olive oil and butter to a dutch oven on the stovetop over medium heat. Allow butter to melt completely. Add onion, celery, and carrot. Stir and cook until onions are translucent and carrots have become soft about 10 minutes.
2. Add tomato paste, minced garlic, and seasonings. Stir and cook for just a minute.
3. Add the flour and stir, soaking up any extra liquid in the dutch oven. Slowly add white wine and whisk to create a thick base. Stir in Worcestershire sauce.
4. Add fish stock 1/2 to 1 cup at a time and stir to maintain a thick base until all the stock is added. Add the bay leaf and thyme leaves. Allow simmering for 25 minutes, stirring occasionally.
5. For a smooth bisque, use an immersion blender here. Stir in heavy cream and chopped lobster meat. Sprinkle with more fresh thyme, lemon zest, and lobster meat for serving.

Nutrition Value

Calories: 224kcal | Carbohydrates: 9g | Protein: 8g | Fat: 16g |

93. Cast Iron Skillet Salmon

Prep Time: 5 minutes Cook Time: 10 minutes

Resting Time: 5 minutes Servings: 2 servings

Ingredients

- Panko crust topping
- 1/2 cup panko style breadcrumbs
- 1 tsp garlic powder
- 1/2 tsp dried basil
- 1/2 tsp dried parsley
- 1 tbsp olive oil
- Salt and pepper to taste
- 6-8 oz salmon fillet
- 1-2 tbsp dijon mustard
- 1 tsp lemon zest
- 1 tbsp olive oil
- 3-4 lemon slices

Instructions

1. Preheat oven to 425 degrees F
2. Place the panko, garlic, basil, and parsley in a small bowl
3. Add 1 tbsp olive oil and mix until well combined, season with salt and pepper to taste. Set aside
4. Place the salmon (skin/bottom side down) on a cutting board or piece of parchment paper.
5. Spread dijon mustard all over the top side of salmon
6. Add lemon zest directly on top of the mustard

7. Press panko mixture directly on top of the mustard layer and press slightly so it sticks to the mustard
8. In a large skillet, heat remaining olive oil over medium-high heat
9. Place salmon (mustard/panko side up) in skillet and let sear for 4-5 minutes without moving
10. Top salmon with lemon slices and move the entire skillet to the oven to bake
11. Cook for additional 6 minutes, until salmon is cooked thru and panko crust, is golden brown
12. Remove from oven and allow to rest for 5 minutes before serving

Nutrition Value

Calories: 294kcal | Carbohydrates: 18g | Protein: 43g | Fat: 9g |

94. Buttered Cod Fish Recipe

Prep Time: 5 Minutes Cook Time: 5 Minutes

Total Time: 10 Minutes Servings: 4 Servings

Ingredients

- 1 1/2 lbs cod fillets
- 6 Tbsp unsalted butter, sliced
- ¼ Tsp garlic powder
- ½ tsp salt
- ¼ tsp ground black pepper
- ¾ tsp ground paprika
- 1 tsp fresh herbs (parsley or cilantro)
- Few lemon slices, drizzle for serving

Instructions

1. Combine the ingredients for the seasoning in a small bowl.
2. Cut cod into smaller pieces, if desired. Season all sides of the cod with seasoning.
3. Heat 2 Tbsp butter in a large skillet over medium-high heat. Once butter melts, add cod to the skillet. Cook 2 minutes.
4. Turn the heat down to medium. Gently flip the cod. Top with remaining butter and cook another 3-4 minutes.
5. Butter will completely melt and the fish will cook. (Don't overcook the cod, it will become mushy and completely fall apart.)
6. Drizzle cod with fresh lemon juice and herbs. Serve immediately.
7. Enjoy, friends.

Nutrition Value

Calories: 294kcal| Protein: 30g| Fat: 18g|

95. Cast Iron Seared Halibut

Total Time: 45 minutes Servings: 4

Ingredients

- 4 halibut fillets (about 7 oz/200 g each)
- 1 tbsp canola oil
- 1 1/2 tsp salt
- 2 tbsp salted butter, softened
- 1/4 cup fresh lemon juice

Instructions

1. Place a 10 inch cast iron frypan on barbecue grid on the natural gas barbecue. Heat frypan over high heat for 15 minutes.
2. Brush both sides of halibut fillets with oil. Sprinkle with salt. 3. Turn barbecue control down to low heat.
3. Place halibut in a frypan on barbecue grid and sear, with the lid down, for 5 minutes. Flip halibut over.
4. Add butter and stir until butter is melted. Add lemon juice and cook, basting halibut frequently with cooking liquid, until fish flakes easily with a fork, about 1 minute. Remove from heat.
5. Serve drizzled with cooking liquid.

Nutritional Value

Calories: 245| Fat: 12.8g| Protein: 31g| Carbohydrate: 1g|

96. Garlic Butter Cod Fish

Servings: 4 Prep Time: 5 Minutes

Cook Time: 10 Minutes Total Time: 15 Minutes

Ingredients

- 1 tbsp olive oil
- 5 small codfish fillets
- 1 tsp. garlic powder
- 1/2 teaspoon onion powder
- 1/4 teaspoon paprika
- Salt and black pepper to taste
- 3 tbsp unsalted butter
- 1 tbsp garlic clove - minced
- 1 tsp lemon zest
- 1 tbsp fresh chopped green onions for garnish

Instructions

1. In a large skillet heat olive oil over medium-high heat. Pat codfish dry with a paper towel and season all over with garlic powder, onion powder, paprika, and salt, and pepper.

2. Place the codfish in a large (10-inch) skillet and turn the heat to medium. Sear fish for 3-4 minutes. Flip your codfish fillets over to cook the other side.

3. Add butter and when it melts, add garlic and lemon zest. Cook for about 1 minute.

4. Gently remove fish from the pan and plate onto a serving dish. Garnish with green onions.

Nutritional Facts

Calories: 190kcal| Carbohydrates: 1g| Protein: 14g| Fat: 15g|

97. Cast Iron Lemon Garlic Salmon

Prep Time: 5 mins Cook Time: 15 mins

Total Time: 20 mins Servings: 2

Ingredients

- 2 fresh salmon filets 5-6 oz each with skin on
- 1 lemon cut in quarters
- 1 tbsp of garlic salt
- 1/2 cup of freshly chopped parsley
- 1/4 cup of butter

Instructions

- Light Charcoals in the charcoal chimney and let burn for 10-15 minutes
- Spread hot coals over grilling area and preheat grill & cast iron pan for approximately 10 minutes.
- On a plate, lather salmon flesh side with garlic salt and squeeze two-quarters of lemon on top. Let salmon sit for 5 minutes before cooking.
- Once the skillet is hot, place all of the butter into the pan and let melt
- Place salmon skin side down into skillet for about 6-8 minutes
- Flip salmon on to flesh side to cook for 2-3 minutes
- Flip salmon back to skin side down and squeeze the last bit of lemon on top
- Place fresh parsley on top and enjoy!

Nutrition Value

Calories: 173kcal | Carbohydrates: 1g | Protein: 23g | Fat: 8g

98. Easy Mediterranean Fish Skillet

Prep Time: 15 mins Cook Time: 15 mins

Total Time: 30 mins Serevings: 4

Ingredients

- 4 6 ounce fish fillets cod or halibut
- 2 Tbsp olive oil
- 1 medium yellow red or green pepper, sliced
- 1/2 large onion, sliced
- 4 large garlic cloves, chopped
- 1 teaspoon dried basil
- 1/4 cup chicken stock
- 1/4 cup white wine
- 1/2 cup cherry tomatoes, halved
- 1/3 cup kalamata olives, pitted
- Salt and pepper
- Garnish with feta, chopped basil, or fresh parsley if desired

Instructions

1. Pat fish dry with a paper towel. Sprinkle liberally with salt and pepper. Slice vegetables and set aside.
2. Heat large cast-iron or nonstick skillet to medium-high heat. Add olive oil and heat for about 30 seconds or until shimmery but not smoking.
3. Add fish to the hot skillet.
4. Sear for 3-4 minutes on each side. When the fish releases from the pan easily it is ready to flip.
5. Remove fish from skillet and set aside.
6. Add peppers and onion to the skillet.
7. Cook 2-3 minutes until slightly soft.
8. Add garlic and tomatoes. Season with salt and pepper.
9. Add basil, white wine, and chicken stock to vegetables in the pan, scraping up all the little bits from the bottom.
10. Add fish back to skillet and continue to cook until cooked through and fish flakes easily. Another 3-4 minutes.
11. Toss kalamata's into the pan until slightly heated.
12. Serve with a sprinkle of feta, fresh basil or fresh parsley, and lemon wedges if desired.

Nutrition Facts

Calories: 284kcal Fat: 8g| Carbohydrates: 5g| Protein: 28g

99. Cast Iron Skillet Seared Salmon Recipe

Prep Time: 5 minutes Cook Time: 15 minutes

Total Time: 20 minutes Servings: 2

Ingredients

- 2 6 oz. Salmon fillets, skin on
- Salt and pepper
- 3 tbsp butter
- 1 garlic clove, minced
- 1 tbsp honey

Instructions

1. Place oven rack 7 or 8 inches from the broiler element and turn on the broiler.
2. Place butter into a cast-iron skillet or other heavy oven-safe skillet and melt over medium heat. Stir the butter around until the milk solids start to caramelize, then lower the heat to low.
3. Keep stirring while the butter starts to get a brown color and you may notice a slightly nutty aroma, (5 or 6 minutes).
4. Stir in the minced garlic cook until fragrant, 30 to 45 seconds. Salt and pepper the salmon, then add to the skillet, skin down.
5. Baste the salmon with the butter using a spoon by tipping the skillet to get a nice spoonful. Do this every minute or so.
6. Cook the salmon until it is nearly halfway cooked through, 7 minutes.
7. Put 1 Tbsp of honey in a small bowl and add a spoonful of hot butter from the skillet. Stir to thin the honey.
8. Drizzle about half of the honey over the top of the salmon fillets. Place the skillet under the broiler.
9. Broil for 2 minutes keeping an eye on the salmon so that the honey does not burn.
10. Remove from the oven and drizzle the salmon with the remaining honey. Cover the skillet with a lid for 2 minutes to finish the cooking and to rest the salmon.
11. Serve right away with lemon if desired.

Nutrition Information

Calories: 342kcal Total Fat: 19g| Carbohydrates: 7g| Protein: 8g

100. Cast-Iron Skillet Coho Salmon Vesuvio

Prep Time: 5 Min Cook Time: 15 Min

Total Time: 20 Min Serves: 4

Ingredients

- 1¼ pounds coho fillet
- 6 cloves garlic
- 2 tsp.s salt
- 2 tsp.s dry thyme, (or 1½ tsp.s fresh)
- 2 tsp.s dry oregano (or 1½ teaspoons fresh)
- 1 Tbsp lemon pepper
- ¼ cup chicken stock
- ¼ cup lemon juice
- 1 tablespoon olive oil
- 2 Tbsp butter

Instructions

1. Mix salt, thyme, oregano, and lemon pepper. The cover fillet in the spice mixture (the entire spice mixture may not be needed).
2. In a cast-iron skillet, heat olive oil. Meanwhile, set oven to 325°. When the oil is hot, place fillet flesh-side down and cook for 2 minutes.
3. Flip salmon skin side down and add stock, lemon juice, and garlic. Spoon the sauce and garlic over the salmon and place in the oven for 10-12 minutes.
4. Remove from oven and place on stovetop over low heat. Add butter and spoon over salmon for a minute or two.
5. Garnish with fresh oregano and thyme and serve warm.

Nutrition Value

Calories: 224kcal | Carbohydrates: 9g | Protein: 8g | Fat: 16g |

VEGETARIAN AND VEGAN

101. Loaded Veggie Skillet

Prep Time: 10 minutes Cook Time: 40 minutes

Total Time: 50 minutes Servings: 4

Ingredients

- 450 g potatoes, scrubbed, skin on, and cut into 2cm cubes I used Maris Piper, but any potato will do.
- 3 tbsp olive oil, divided
- ½ tsp sea salt, divided
- ½ tsp cracked black pepper, divided
- 1 small onion, (100g) cut in half then thinly sliced
- 1 medium green bell pepper (110g) pith and seeds removed then thinly sliced
- 1 medium red bell pepper (110g) pith and seeds removed then thinly sliced
- 230 g portobello mushroom (3 large mushrooms) wiped clean then sliced
- 1 tsp dried oregano
- 2 cloves of garlic minced
- A scant ¼ tsp dried red chili flakes optional
- 90 g spinach
- 4 large eggs
- 2 tbsp freshly squeezed lemon juice

Instructions

1. Preheat the oven to 200 degrees C, 392F. I use an electric fan-assisted oven, please adjust according to your oven.
2. Place the potatoes on a baking tray, pour over 2 Tbsp of oil add ¼ teaspoon each of salt and black pepper. Toss well then bake in the oven for 30 minutes turning the potatoes halfway through cooking.
3. While the potatoes are roasting, cook up the veggies.
4. Heat the remaining oil in a skillet, add the onion and cook over medium heat until soft, about 10 minutes.
5. Add the peppers and cook for 5 minutes. Once the peppers are a little soft add the mushrooms, garlic, oregano, salt, pepper, and chili flakes. Cook for another 5 minutes.
6. Now add the spinach, I add half first, let that wilt down then add the remaining spinach. Add the lemon juice and stir well.
7. Once the potatoes are cooked transfer them to the skillet and give everything a good stir. Check the seasoning now and add more if necessary.
8. Make 4 little wells in the skillet, break one egg into each well. Place a lid over the skillet, this will help cook your eggs quicker. Once the eggs are cooked to your taste turn off the heat.
9. Sprinkle over the parsley and chopped spring onion and serve.
10. Serve with lemon wedges and more red chili flakes if you like.

Nutrition Value

Calories: 289kcal | Carbohydrates: 27g | Protein: 11.4g | Fat: 15.9g

102. Vegan Enchiladas Skillet

Prep Time: 15 minutes Cook Time: 15 minutes

Total Time: 30 minutes Servings: 4 servings

Ingredients

- 2 Tbsp oil divided
- 10 small corn tortillas cut into strips
- ½ large red onion diced
- 2-3 cloves garlic minced
- 1 small butternut squash peeled and cut into ½" cubes
- 1 ½ teaspoon chili powder
- ½ tsp. cumin
- ½ tsp. paprika
- ½ teaspoon salt
- 1 can black beans, drained and rinsed
- ½ cup corn frozen or canned
- 1 cup crushed tomatoes
- 10 ounces enchiladas sauce
- 4 large kale leaves chopped small
- Salt and pepper to taste
- A few springs of cilantro chopped
- 1 jalapeño diced
- 2 green onions diced
- 1 avocado

Instructions

1. In a large cast-iron skillet heat 1 tablespoon of oil. Add tortilla strips and cook, stirring often, for 5 minutes, until lightly crispy and browned.
2. Transfer to a paper towel.
3. Add the remaining oil and sauté onions for 5 minutes, stirring frequently, until onions are translucent and fragrant.
4. Add the garlic and sauté for 30 more seconds.
5. Add the butternut squash, chili powder, cumin, paprika, and salt. Stir to coat then reduce heat to low and cover.
6. Cook until the squash is tender. About 5 minutes.
7. Add the black beans, corn, tomatoes, enchiladas sauce, and kale.
8. Cook for an additional 3 minutes until kale is wilted. Season with salt and pepper.
9. Stir in corn tortillas and bring to a simmer, simmering for about 10 minutes until the liquid has boiled down.
10. Remove enchiladas from heat and let set up 10 additional minutes before serving.
11. Top with jalapeño, cilantro, and green onions.

Nutrition Value

Calories: 447kcal | Carbohydrates: 71g | Protein: 11g | Fat: 17g

103. Vegetarian Taco Skillet

Prep Time: 10 Mins Cook Time: 25 Mins

Total Time: 35 Mins Servings: 4

Ingredients

- 1 Tbsp olive oil
- 1 onion chopped
- 1 red bell pepper, stemmed, seeds removed and chopped
- 3 cloves garlic, chopped
- 1 cup quinoa, rinsed
- 2 cups vegetable broth
- 15 oz fire-roasted tomatoes
- 4 oz mild green chiles
- 3 teaspoons chili powder
- 2 tsp.s ground cumin

- 3/4 tsp. smoked paprika
- 1/2 teaspoon dried oregano
- 1 tsp. kosher salt
- 1/4 teaspoon black pepper
- 15 oz black beans, rinsed and drained
- 1 cup frozen corn
- 1/4 cup chopped cilantro
- 1 1/2 cups shredded Mexican blend or cheddar cheese
- Optional toppings: sliced green onions, avocado, cilantro, tomatoes
- Tortilla chips, salsa, or pico de gallo, for serving

Instructions

1. In a large skillet, heat the olive oil over medium-high heat.
2. Add the onion and bell pepper; cook for 5 minutes or until tender, stirring occasionally.
3. Add the garlic and cook for one minute.
4. Add the quinoa, vegetable broth, tomatoes, green chilies, chili powder, cumin, paprika, oregano, salt, and pepper. Stir until combined and let come to a boil.
5. Reduce heat to low and cover with a lid. If your pan doesn't have a lid you can cover it with a baking sheet. Simmer for 15 to 18 minutes or until the quinoa is cooked.
6. Remove the lid and stir in the black beans, corn, and cilantro. Top with shredded cheese and put the lid back on for 3 to 5 minutes or until the cheese is melted.
7. Top with green onions, avocado, cilantro, and diced tomatoes.
8. Spoon onto plates and serve warm with tortilla chips and salsa or pico de gallo. Season with additional salt and pepper, if necessary.

Nutritional Value

Calories: 406kcal| Carbohydrates: 48g| Protein: 20g| Fat: 13g|

104. Make-Ahead Vegan Cinnamon Rolls

Prep Time: 55 Minutes Cook Time: 25 Minutes

Additional Time: 2 Hours Servings: 4

Ingredients

- 2 Tbsp ground flaxseed
- 1/3 cup warm water
- 4 cups all-purpose flour, divided, plus more for kneading and rolling
- 1/2 cup True Goodness Cane Sugar
- 1 Tbsp active dry yeast (or two packets)
- 1 teaspoon salt
- 1 cup unsweetened almond, coconut, or other plant-based milk
- 1/3 cup plant-based butter (like Pure Blends Plant-Based Butter made with Coconut Oil)
- 1 cup packed light brown sugar
- 2 Tbsp True Goodness Organic Ground Cinnamon
- 1/2 cup plant-based butter (like Pure Blends Plant-Based Butter made with Coconut Oil)
- 1/4 cup plant-based butter (like Pure Blends Plant-Based Butter made with Coconut Oil)
- 4 ounces plant-based cream cheese
- 1 1/2 cups powdered sugar
- 2 tsp.s vanilla extract
- Zest and juice of one orange, optional

Instructions

1. In a small bowl, whisk together the flaxseed and warm water until well combined, set aside to thicken.
2. In a large bowl, combine 2 cups of flour, sugar, yeast, and salt. Set aside.
3. In a small saucepan over medium-low heat, combine the plant-based milk and 1/3 cup of a plant-based butter. Heat until warm and the butter is melted. Pour into the flour mixture, add the flax mixture, and stir until well-combined (it should be on the wet side). Stir in an additional 1 cup of flour.
4. Turn out the dough onto a floured surface, and knead in the additional 1 cup of flour. Continue kneading until the dough is very soft and pliable, about five minutes—depending on humidity that day, you might need to add more flour to keep the dough from being too sticky. Transfer the dough to a clean, well-oiled boil, cover, and let rise in a warm spot until doubled in size, about one hour.
5. Meanwhile, grease one 9 x 13-inch baking pan, two 8-inch cake pans, or two 10-inch cast-iron skillets, set aside.
6. In a small bowl, begin making the filling by combining the brown sugar and cinnamon, set aside.
7. On a floured surface, roll out the dough into a rectangle approximately 20" x 16" in size. Spread with the plant-based butter for the filling, then sprinkle liberally with the brown sugar and cinnamon mixture.
8. Roll the dough up lengthwise, pinching the seam closed when finished. Use your hands to gently squeeze the tube to even it out, seal it together, and stretch it out a bit.
9. Using a bit of unflavored dental floss or a very sharp knife, cut off both ragged ends (you can bake these, but they just aren't as pretty!), and slice the remaining roll into 12 even slices. Arrange in a prepared baking

dish(es). Cover and let rise in a warm spot until noticeably puffier, about an hour.

10. Meanwhile, make the frosting by creaming together the plant-based butter and vegan cream cheese using a hand mixer or whisk. Add in the powdered sugar, vanilla, orange juice, and zest, and mix until very smooth and creamy. Cover and set aside.

11. Preheat oven to 350°F. Bake pan(s), uncovered, for about 20 minutes or until the tops are golden brown. Let cool for about five minutes, then drizzle on the frosting liberally. Serve immediately.

Nutrition Information

Calories: 224kcal Total Fat: 29g| Carbohydrates: 82g| Protein: 9g

105. Skillet Root Vegetable

Prep Time: 20 mins Cook Time: 40 mins

Servings: 6

Ingredients

- 2 tbsp avocado oil
- 1 medium sweet potato, cubed
- 1/2 red onion, cut into cubes
- 3 cups butternut squash cubes
- 1 delicata squash, cut into 1/2" pieces
- 1/2 -1 tsp salt
- 1/2 tsp thyme
- 1/2 tsp rosemary

Instructions

1. Preheat oven to 400 F (Roast).

2. Place cut vegetables into a bowl and add oil. Add spices and salt. Mix to combine. If vegetables are not coated, add one more TBSP avocado oil.

3. Place in preheated oven for 20 minutes. Using hot pads again, remove and stir vegetables. Heat for another 15 minutes and check for doneness. Let cool before serving. Add fresh rosemary to the final dish if desired.

Nutrition Facts

Calories: 314kcal Fat: 5g| Carbohydrates: 28g| Fiber: 4g| Protein: 2g|

106. Easy Vegan Sautéed Vegetables

Prep Time: 15 Minutes Cook Time: 10 Minutes

Servings: 4

Ingredients

- 1 tablespoon olive oil see notes below for preparing without oil
- ½ red onion chopped
- 1 cup zucchini cut into small pieces
- 1 cup summer squash cut into small pieces
- 1 cup yellow squash cut into small pieces
- 1 cup green beans end removed, cut in thirds
- ½ bell pepper red, yellow or orange – cut in thin strips
- 1 cup tomatoes cherry tomatoes – halved
- ½ teaspoon dried herbs or Italian seasoning I used Spike all-purpose seasoning in this recipe
- ½ teaspoon sea salt
- ¼ tsp. black pepper freshly ground

Instructions

1. Wash and slice your vegetables. Once your veggies are prepped, blot them dry with a clean towel.

2. Place skillet on the stove over medium-high heat. Test the temperature of your heated skillet by sprinkling a few drops of water into the pan. If the water sizzles the pan is ready.

3. Pour a very small amount of extra virgin olive oil into the bottom of the pan. Use only enough to lightly coat the pan – about a Tbsp or less.

4. Don't overheat the oil as you don't want it to smoke or burn. See notes below for sautéing without oil.

5. Carefully place sliced veggies into the pan.

6. I suggest adding them in this order:

7. Onions 2. Green Beans 3. Bell Peppers 4. Zucchini and Squash 5. Tomatoes.

8. Try not to overcrowd them. Be sure to leave room for the juices to evaporate. If your pan isn't large enough, it's better to sauté them in batches than to try to do them all at once.

9. While the veggies are cooking add your dry seasonings. salt & pepper. Stir to combine.

10. Turn or flip veggies with a heatproof spatula or tongs about once a minute. Sauté until the veggies are slightly browned and tender – about 8-10 minutes. Be careful not to overcook them. Remove from heat.

11. Serve hot and enjoy!

Nutritional Value

Calories: 63kcal | Carbohydrates: 7g | Protein: 2g | Fat: 4g |

107. Southwest Veggie Skillet

Prep Time: 15 minutes Cook Time: 25 minutes

Total Time: 40 minutes Servings: 4

Ingredients

Vegetarian Breakfast Skillet

- 1 tablespoon olive oil
- 1 pound baby red potatoes, cut into 1 inch chunks
- 1 yellow onion, chopped
- 1 green bell pepper, chopped
- Coarse kosher salt and freshly ground black pepper
- 1 tsp. chili powder
- 1 Roma tomato, seeds removed, diced
- 15 ounces canned pinto beans, rinsed and drained
- ⅓ cup salsa
- ½ cup shredded cheddar jack cheese
- Freshly chopped cilantro, optional
- Sliced avocado, optional
- Hot sauce or extra salsa, optional

Fried Eggs

- 1 Tbsp olive oil, divided
- 4 eggs
- Coarse kosher salt and freshly ground black pepper

Instructions

Vegetarian Breakfast Skillet

1. Heat olive oil in a large cast-iron skillet over medium heat. Once hot, add the potatoes, onion, and bell pepper. Season with salt and pepper and cook, stirring frequently, until the potatoes are softened, about 20 minutes.

2. Add the chili powder and stir to combine, letting it cook for about 1 minute more.

3. Add tomato, salsa, and pinto beans, and let cook, stirring occasionally until warmed through, about 5 minutes.

4. Top with cheese and let rest a few minutes until melted.

5. Serve the breakfast skillet topped with fried eggs, sliced avocado, a sprinkle of cilantro, and a dash of hot sauce or salsa.

Fried Eggs

1. While the cheese is melting on the breakfast skillet, heat ½ Tbsp olive oil in a small skillet over medium-low heat. Once hot, cook the eggs one or two at a time.

2. For sunny side up eggs, cover the pan with a lid and let cook on one side until the whites are solid but the yolk is still jiggly about 2-3 minutes.

3. Remove the eggs from the skillet, season with salt and pepper, and repeat with the remaining eggs.

Nutritional Value

Calories: 371kcal | Carbohydrates: 41g | Protein: 17g | Fat: 16g |

108. Easy Potato Skillet Breakfast

Prep Time: 15 mins Cook Time: 45 mins

Total Time: 1 hr Servings: 5 servings

Ingredients

- 1 and ¼ pounds russet potatoes, medium diced (skins on)
- 1 and ¼ pounds red potatoes, medium diced (skins on)
- 1 Tbsp canola oil
- 1 tsp. cumin
- ½ teaspoon chili powder
- ¼ teaspoon salt
- 1 red bell pepper, diced
- 1 green bell pepper, diced
- 1 large yellow onion, diced
- 1 jalapeno, minced
- 3 cloves garlic, minced
- 1 can (15.7 ounces) black beans, drained and rinsed (about 1.5 cups)
- 1 bunch (12 ounces) spinach, stems removed
- 2 small avocados, for topping
- Cilantro, for topping

Instructions

1. Preheat the oven to 425° F.

2. In a large cast-iron or other oven-safe pan, heat 1 tablespoon of canola oil over medium heat. Once hot, add the diced potatoes, cumin, chili powder, and salt. Stir to evenly coat, cooking for just 2 minutes.

3. Put the cast iron pan in the preheated oven for 20 minutes, stirring halfway through.

4. After 20 minutes, add the bell pepper, onion, jalapenos, and garlic. Cook another 15 minutes, stirring halfway through. After 15 minutes, return the cast iron to the stove.

5. Saute on the stove over medium heat until the potatoes are lightly browned and fully cooked through. Stir in the black beans and spinach. The skillet breakfast is ready once the black beans are heated through and the spinach is wilted.

6. Top with avocado and cilantro. Portion into separate containers for a week of breakfast meal prep. Enjoy!

Nutritional Value

Calories: 224kcal Carbohydrates: 70g| Protein: 13g| Fat: 9g

109. Vegan Skillet Apple Pie

Prep Time: 20 minutes Cook Time: 45 minutes

Total Time: 1 hour 5 minutes Servings: 12 servings

Ingredients

- 2 and ¾ cups all-purpose flour
- 2 vegan buttery sticks of 8 Tbsp each, or substitute half with shortening (trans-fat-free)
- 1 tablespoon turbinado or vegan cane sugar
- Ice cold water
- 7-8 Golden Delicious apples, cored and sliced into ¼-inch-thick slices (or use any apples suited to make pies)
- ½ cup turbinado or vegan cane sugar
- 1 Tbsp molasses (optional, but adds great flavor)
- 2 tsp. cinnamon
- 1 teaspoon dry ginger
- 1 tsp. nutmeg
- ¼ teaspoon salt
- Juice of 1 lemon
- 2 tablespoon cornstarch

Instructions

1. Mix the flour and sugar in a bowl.

2. Cut the butter into ¼-inch cubes and add to the flour. Using a pastry cutter or a fork, "cut" the butter into the flour until you have small pieces of butter evenly dispersed through the flour.

3. Drizzle ice-cold water into the dough, a little at a time, mixing with a fork, until the dough is moist enough to hold together.

4. Divide the dough into two, and shape each half into a disc. Wrap tightly in cling wrap and refrigerate for at least 30 minutes or as much as 2 days. If making well in advance, freeze and thaw completely before using.

5. Place all the ingredients for the filling in a large bowl. Mix thoroughly and let the filling stand at least 30 minutes before baking. You can also make the filling the day before and refrigerate.

Assemble And Bake The Pie:

1. Preheat the oven to 425 degrees.

2. Roll out one of the crusts so it's big enough to fit into a 9-inch cast-iron skillet. Place the crust into the skillet and fit it to the sides. Refrigerate until you make the top crust.

3. Roll out the other crust to a diameter about 2 inches wider than the top of the cast-iron skillet. You need to make vents in the upper crust for steam to escape while baking. You can either do this with a knife after you place the top crust on the filling or, if you want to cut a decorative shape with a cookie cutter (I cut a star), do it before placing the crust on the filling.

4. Pour the apple filling and any juices into the bottom crust in the skillet. Then fold the top crust in half and carefully transfer to the skillet, covering the filling completely. Fold in any overhanging dough and crimp with your fingers or with a fork for a decorative edge, and to seal in the apples.

5. For a golden crust, brush on a mixture of 1 Tbsp oil and 1 Tbsp of nondairy milk on the top crust.

6. Bake in the oven for 45 minutes or until the top is golden brown.

7. Let the pie cool thoroughly on a rack before cutting into it. Exercise care when you handle the hot iron skillet because it is heavy and extremely hot. Make sure you wear oven mitts at all times when handling it before it cools down thoroughly.

Nutritional Value

Calories: 302kcal | Fat: 15g |

110. Vegetarian Chili

Prep Time: 10 minutes Cook Time: 25 minutes

Servings: 2

Ingredients

- 1 cup Kidney Beans cooked
- 1 cup Chickpeas cooked
- 2 cloves Garlic diced
- 2 stalks celery diced
- 1 Yellow Bell Pepper finely diced
- 1 Yellow Onion finely diced
- 1/2 cup Sweet Corn Kernels cooked
- 3/4 cup Vegetable Broth
- 1 tbsp Tomato Paste
- 1 can Dice Tomato withh their juices
- 1 tsp Smoked Paprika
- 1 tsp Ground Cumin
- 1 tbsp Lemon Juice freshly squeezed
- Salt and Freshly ground Pepper to taste
- Garnishing
- Avocado chopped
- Cilantro fresh

Instructions

1. Heat a non-stick pot or skillet and fry the garlic and onion over medium-high heat until translucent, stirring frequently.
2. Add the bell pepper, the celery and cook for a few minutes, stirring frequently.
3. Add the smoked paprika and cumin, stir to combine.
4. Add the sweet corn, chickpeas, kidney beans, tomato paste and diced tomatoes, the vegetable broth, and stir to combine.
5. Bring to boil over medium heat, then simmer uncovered over low heat for 20 minutes, until it thickens.
6. Season with salt to taste, add the lemon juice, and stir to combine.
7. Serve warm, topped with avocado and fresh cilantro, on its own or with rice or quinoa.

Nutritional Value

Calories: 387kcal | Carbohydrates: 74g | Protein: 20g | Fat: 4g |

111. Bacon and Sweet Potato Veggie

Active Time: 20 Mins Total Time: 25 Mins

Servings: Serves 2

Ingredients

- 3 center-cut bacon slices, diced
- 1/2 cup diced onions
- 2 garlic cloves, minced
- 1/3 cup diced yellow bell pepper
- 1/3 cup diced red bell pepper
- 1 cup (1/2-in.) cubed sweet potato
- 1/8 teaspoon kosher salt
- 1/8 tsp. crushed red pepper
- 1/4 cup unsalted chicken stock
- 4 ounces fresh spinach
- 1-ounce feta cheese, crumbled (about 1/4 cup)

Instructions

1. Place bacon in a large cast-iron skillet over medium heat; cook 5 minutes or until just starting to crisp. Add onion; sauté for 3 minutes.
2. Add garlic; sauté 1 minute.

3. Add bell peppers; sauté for 4 minutes. Add potato, salt, crushed red pepper, and stock.
4. Cover and cook for 9 minutes or until potatoes are tender.
5. Add spinach; cook, uncovered, 1 minute or until spinach wilts.
6. Divide the mixture between 2 bowls; sprinkle with cheese.

Nutritional Information

Calories: 177| Fat: 5.5g| Protein: 9g| Carbohydrate: 24g| Fiber: 5g|

112. Dutch Oven Vegetable Stew

Prep Time: 5 minutes Cook Time: 25 minutes

Total Time: 30 minutes 4 servings

Ingredients

- 2 Tbsp oil
- 8 oz mushrooms, halved or quartered
- 1 teaspoon salt
- 1 small onion, chopped
- 2 large carrots, sliced
- 1 celery stick, sliced
- 8-10 baby potatoes, cubed
- 2 cloves garlic, minced
- 1 tablespoon tomato paste
- 2 Tbsp flour
- ½ cup red wine
- 1 Tbsp liquid aminos, or soy sauce
- 2 cups vegetable stock
- 1 teaspoon thyme
- 1 bay leaf

Instructions

1. Heat 1 tablespoon oil in a large pot. Add the mushrooms and saute until browned, about 5 minutes. Add the onion, carrot, celery, potatoes, and salt and saute for 2-3 minutes.
2. Add garlic and tomato paste and saute 1 minute more.
3. Adding the flour. Stir to coat the vegetables in the flour, then add the red wine and liquid aminos or soy sauce.
4. Simmer until the red wine has almost entirely evaporated. Add vegetable stock, thyme, and bay leaf.
5. Cover and simmer for 10 minutes, then uncover to let the stew thicken a bit, about 10 minutes.
6. Once the vegetables are tender, check the seasoning and divide among bowls. Enjoy!

Nutrition Value

Calories: 330kcal | Carbohydrates: 47g | Protein: 6g | Fat: 14g

113. Vegetarian Pasta Bake

Prep Time: 15 minutes Cook Time: 45 minutes

Total Time: 1 hour Servings: 8

Ingredients

- 1 lb pasta
- Kosher salt
- 3 tbsp olive oil divided
- 8 oz mushrooms white button, sliced
- black pepper freshly ground
- 1 cup onion chopped, 1 medium-sized onion
- 1 cup celery chopped, about 2 stalks
- 1 cup carrots chopped, about 2 small carrots
- 3 cloves garlic minced
- 1 lb OZO Plant-Based Ground thawed
- ¼ cup red wine
- 2 tbsp tomato paste
- 1 28 oz. can whole tomatoes drained, San Marzano, are best
- 1 15 oz. can tomato sauce
- 1 tbsp oregano dried
- 8 oz Mozzarella shredded
- ¼ cup Parmesan cheese grated
- 2 tbsp parsley fresh, chopped, optional

Instructions

1. Preheat oven to 350°F. Bring a pot of salted water to a boil.
2. Add the pasta to the boiling water and follow package instructions to cook until al dente.
3. Heat 2 tbsp of oil over medium heat in a large cast-iron skillet (or large skillet if baking the pasta in a baking dish). Add the mushrooms and sauté until soft and starting to slightly brown on the edges. Sprinkle with a

little salt and pepper. Transfer the mushrooms to a bowl and set them aside.
4. In the same pan, still over medium heat, add another tbsp of oil. Add the onion, celery, and carrot, and sauté until soft, about 5 minutes. Add the garlic and sauté for another minute.
5. Add the OZO Plant-Based Ground and cook for 5 minutes, stirring occasionally. Season with ¾ tsp salt and ½ tsp pepper.
6. Add the wine into the pan and simmer until reduced, about 4 minutes.
7. Stir in the tomato paste and continue stirring until fully incorporated.
8. Use your hands to squeeze the whole tomatoes into the pan. Stir in the sautéd mushrooms, tomato sauce, and oregano. Simmer for another 5 minutes. Taste and add more salt, if needed.
9. Drain the pasta and mix it into the pan with the sauce. If using a baking dish, transfer the pasta with sauce into it.
10. Sprinkle the mozzarella over the pasta and then top with the grated Parmesan.
11. Bake for 25 to 30 minutes, or until lightly browned on top and the sides are bubbling. Remove from the oven and let rest for 5 minutes. Garnish with chopped parsley and additional grated Parmesan, if desired. Serve at once.

Nutritional Value

Calories: 390kcal | Carbohydrates: 50g | Protein: 16g | Fat: 10g

114. Vegan Mediterranean Breakfast Skillet

Cook Time: 12 Min Prep Time: 10 Min

Servings: 5

Ingredients

- 1 package (16 Ounces) Beyond Beef
- 1 can artichoke hearts, drained
- 1/2 cup tomatoes, cherry, sliced
- 1 can chickpeas, drained
- 1/2 cup sweet potato, small diced
- 1 yellow onion, sliced thin
- 2 garlic cloves, minced
- 10 each, kalamata olives, minced
- 1 tablespoon coriander
- 1 Tbsp rosemary (fresh or dried)
- 1 Tbsp oregano (fresh or dried)
- 2 Tbsp nutritional yeast
- 1 Tbsp paprika

Instructions

1. Heat a medium cast-iron pan or skillet over medium heat.
2. Add chickpeas, sweet potato, garlic, and onion; sauté for 5 minutes, stirring often.
3. Deglaze the pan with lemon juice then crumble in the Beyond Meat.
4. Cook for 5 minutes until lightly browned then mix in the coriander, nutritional yeast, artichoke hearts, and tomatoes. Sauté on medium-high heat for 5 more minutes. Then turn off the heat.
5. Mix in the olives and fresh herbs then dig in!

Nutrition Facts

Total Fat: 18g| Total Carbohydrates: 28g| Protein: 22g

115. Charred Summer Vegetables

Prep Time: 10 Minutes Cook Time: 20 Minutes

Total Time: 30 Minutes Servings: 6 Servings

Ingredients

- 2 Tbsp grapeseed or olive oil
- 2 large shallots, finely chopped
- 1 red bell pepper, chopped
- 2 cups green beans, trimmed and chopped
- 2 ears corn, kernels removed
- 1 zucchini squash, chopped
- 1 yellow squash, chopped
- 1 teaspoon ground cumin
- 1 teaspoon dried basil
- ¼ tsp. salt, or to taste
- 2 Tbsp fresh lemon juice
- 2 Tbsp fresh parsley, chopped

Instructions

1. In a 10-inch cast-iron skillet, heat the oil to medium and add the chopped shallots and bell pepper.

2. Sauté 2 to 3 minutes until very fragrant, then add the green beans and corn kernels.
3. Continue sautéing until shallots and bell pepper are softened, about 5 minutes.
4. Add the zucchini, yellow squash, ground cumin, dried basil, and salt and stir well to incorporate.
5. Cover, and cook an additional 5 minutes, or until vegetables have reached the desired level of doneness.
6. Remove skillet from heat, stir in the lemon juice and parsley and serve.

Nutritional Value

Calories: 447kcal | Carbohydrates: 71g | Protein: 11g | Fat: 17g |

116. Campfire Lasagna (Vegetarian)

Prep Time: 15 mins Cook Time: 30 mins

Total Time: 45 mins Servings: 4

Ingredients

- 1 package no-boil lasagna noodles
- 15-ounce full-fat ricotta cheese
- 2 cups shredded mozzarella (fresh preferred), divided
- 15 ounce can spinach, drained (reserve liquid)
- 28-ounce jar pasta sauce
- 1 teaspoon salt
- 2 Tbsp Italian seasoning or use your favorite herb mixture (such as Herbs de Provence)

Instructions

1. Preheat campfire coals until very hot. Once coals are hot, set aside around 15 coals aside for easy access (you'll be setting them on top of your Dutch oven).
2. Meanwhile, mix ricotta, 1 ½ cups mozzarella, spinach, salt, and herb mixture. Taste and add more seasoning if necessary.
3. Add ⅓ of the cheese mixture to the bottom of the Dutch oven and spread it out to cover the pot.
4. Add ⅓ Cheese + Spinach Mixture to Dutch Oven.
5. Top cheese with ⅓ of the pasta sauce.
6. Add one layer of lasagna noodles. Break noodles as necessary to fit into the round pot. Repeat twice with the remaining spinach cheese mixture, pasta sauce, and noodles (you may have some noodles leftover).
7. Add ⅓ Pasta Sauce + Noodles.
8. Pour reserved liquid from the spinach can into a measuring cup, and add water until you have ¾ cup of liquid total. Pour liquid into lasagna along the edge. Top mixture with remaining mozzarella cheese.
9. Top the Lasagna with Cheese.
10. Place the lid on the Dutch oven. (If your Dutch oven is not a campfire-style oven with a flat lid, you'll need to set the lid on upside down so it can hold the coals.)
11. Place Dutch oven directly on the main batch of coals. Using tongs, set reserved coals on top of the lid, and let it bake for about 25 minutes.
12. Place Dutch Oven on Coals + Top with More Coals.
13. Next, remove the lid, and leave the dutch oven on the fire uncovered for about 5 more minutes. The excess liquid should be boiled off. If needed, let it cook for a few more minutes until any extra liquid has thickened.
14. Campfire Lasagna in a Dutch Oven After Baking
15. Remove Dutch oven from heat. Allow lasagna to cool slightly before serving.
16. Spinach Campfire Lasagna on a Plate.

Nutritional Value

Calories: 341kcal | Carbohydrates: 24g | Protein: 20g | Fat: 18g |

117. Vegetarian Skillet Tortilla Casserole

Ready in: 30mins Prep time: 15mins

Cooking time: 15mins Serves: 8

Ingredients

- 1 bunch green onions
- 1 (15.5 oz) can Nature's Promise Organic No-Salt-Added Black Beans
- 1 (16 oz) can fat-free vegetarian refried beans
- 1 tbsp chili powder
- 2 cups fresh corn kernels
- 2 large tomatoes
- 1 (16 oz) bag shredded Mexican-blend cheeses
- Cooking spray
- 4 burrito-size (about 9–10 inches) flour tortillas
- 1 small romaine heart

Instructions

1. Set one half of grill to high and another half to medium-low.
2. Thinly slice the green onions and drain the black beans. In a large bowl, combine the refried beans, black beans, chili powder, and corn. Fold in sliced green onions.
3. Thinly slice the tomatoes. Reserve ¼ cup of the cheese.
4. Coat the bottom of a 10-inch cast-iron skillet with the cooking spray. Place 1 tortilla on the bottom and top with ⅓ of bean mixture, ⅓ of the tomatoes, then ⅓ of the cheese.
5. Repeat layering with 2 more tortillas, remaining beans, remaining tomatoes, and cheese.
6. Finish with remaining tortilla and reserved ¼ cup cheese.
7. Place the skillet on the cooler side of the grill. Cover and cook 15 min., until center, is hot, rotating skillet once halfway through.
8. Meanwhile, thinly slice the romaine. Garnish the casserole with romaine.

Nutrition Information

Calories: 449kcal| Fat: 20.0g| Saturated Fat: 10.4g| Carbs: 45.2g|

118. Vegan Skillet Cookie

Prep Time: 10 Mins Cook Time: 25 Mins

Total Time: 35 Mins Servings: 10

Ingredients

- 450 g plain white flour
- 1 1/2 tsp baking powder
- 1 tsp bicarbonate of soda
- 1/4 tsp fine sea salt
- 200 g vegan butter, melted
- 100 g soft light brown sugar
- 100 g soft dark brown sugar
- 150 g granulated sugar
- 150 ml soy milk
- 2 tsp vanilla extract
- 2 tsp psyllium husk powder
- 340 g dark chocolate chips
- Pinch flaky sea salt

Instructions

1. Grease a cast-iron skillet with a little vegan butter. Preheat the oven to 160c/320f (fan).
2. In a medium bowl, sieve together the flour, baking powder, baking soda, and fine sea salt.
3. In the bowl of a stand mixer fitted with the paddle attachment, combine the melted vegan butter and sugars. In a measuring jug, whisk together the soy milk, vanilla, and psyllium husk powder. Immediately add to the stand mixer and beat on medium speed for 2 minutes.
4. Add the flour mixture and beat briefly to combine. Finally add the dark chocolate chips, reserving a small handful for topping the cookie.
5. Beat briefly to combine.
6. Spread the cookie dough into the skillet and gently push it into the corners. Top with the last few chocolate chips and sprinkle with the flaky sea salt.
7. Place in the oven and bake for 25 minutes.
8. Remove from the oven and allow to cool for 10 minutes before serving with a big scoop of vegan ice cream.

Nutritional Value

Calories: 636kcal| Carbohydrates: 90g| Protein: 8g| Fat: 28g

119. Vegan Shakshuka

Prep Time: 10 Minutes Cook Time: 15 Minutes

Total Time: 25 Minutes Servings: 2–4 Servings

Ingredients

- 1 tbsp avocado oil (can sub vegetable oil)
- 1/2 onion, chopped
- 2 garlic cloves, chopped
- 1 red pepper, chopped
- 1 cup uncooked quinoa
- 1/2 cup white beans
- 2 cups crushed tomatoes
- 1/4 cup water or vegetable stock
- 2 tsp smoked paprika
- 2 tsp chili powder
- 1 tsp cumin powder

- 1 tsp pomegranate molasses or maple syrup
- Pinch of cayenne pepper
- Salt & pepper to taste
- Cilantro to top

Instructions

1. Cook the quinoa according to package directions. Set aside.
2. Heat the oil in a skillet on medium-high heat then add the onions and garlic letting cook for 2 minutes.
3. Then add the peppers and let them cook on medium heat for another 3-4 minutes until the peppers start to get tender.
4. Lower the heat to medium and add cooked quinoa, white beans, crushed tomatoes, water, smoked paprika, chili powder, cumin, maple syrup, cayenne, salt, and pepper and mix everything.
5. Let cook on low for 10 minutes stirring every few minutes. Taste and adjust seasoning if necessary before serving.

Nutritional Value

Calories: 246kcal Fat: 5g| Carbohydrates: 52g|Protein: 16g

120. Cast Iron Skillet Vegetable Lasagna

Prep Time: 15 Mins Cook Time: 30 Mins

Total Time: 45 Mins Servings: 4

Ingredients

- 6 cloves garlic
- 1 onion
- 1 bell pepper
- 1 8 oz. Package mushrooms
- 1 cup fresh spinach
- Pinch kosher salt
- Pinch pepper
- 1 tbsp. Olive oil
- 1 24 oz. Jar marinara sauce
- 2 cups low sodium vegetable broth
- 1 package lasagna noodles
- ½-3/4 cup ricotta cheese
- ½-3/4 cup mozzarella cheese
- ¼ cup parmesan cheese optional
- 2 tsp. Red chili flakes optional
- ½ cup chopped basil optional

Instructions

1. Mince 6 cloves of garlic and 1 onion.
2. Dice 1 bell pepper and cut 1 8 oz. package button mushrooms into small slices.
3. Roughly chop 1 cup fresh spinach.
4. Heat a large cast-iron skillet to medium. Add 1 Tbsp. olive oil.
5. Once the oil is heated, add the garlic and onions and saute for 2-3 minutes, stirring often.
6. Add the sliced mushrooms along with a pinch of salt and pepper. Saute the mushrooms for 4-5 minutes, stirring often. The mushrooms will cook down quite a bit.
7. Add the diced pepper to the mushrooms and saute for an additional 3-4 minutes, stirring often.
8. Add 1 24 oz. jar of marinara sauce and 1 ½ cups of vegetable broth to the mushrooms and peppers. Stir to combine.
9. Break 8-10 dry lasagna noodles into small pieces and add to the pan. Stir the noodles into the sauce. The noodles cook in the sauce so all the noodles must be submerged in the liquid.
10. Bring the sauce to a low boil and then reduce to a simmer. The sauce should bubble slightly as it cooks. The heat should be hot enough to cook the noodles but not hot enough to cause the sauce to splatter - Medium/low should work fine.
11. Cook the noodles on a low boil for 30 minutes. Stir the noodles every 5 minutes or so (more important toward the 30-minute mark) to prevent them from sticking to the pan. Add ½ cup of vegetable stock as the noodles cook.
12. Once the noodles are cooked and have absorbed most of the sauce, add the cup of chopped spinach and stir into the lasagna.
13. Turn the oven broiler on.
14. Spoon a ½-3/4 cup of ricotta cheese on top of the lasagna in chunks (do not stir ricotta into lasagna) and sprinkle ½-3/4 cup shredded mozzarella on top of the ricotta.

15. Place the pan in the oven directly under the broiler for 2 minutes or until the cheese melts. Remove pan from oven.

16. To Serve: Sprinkle ¼ cup Parmesan cheese, 2 tsp. red chili flakes, and ½ cup chopped fresh basil on top of lasagna (optional).

Nutritional Value

Calories: 396kcal Fat: 4g| Carbohydrates: 54g |Protein: 17g

121. Vegan Savory Skillet Stew With Baby Potato

Prep Time: 20 minutes Cook Time: 35 minutes

Total Time: 50 minutes Servings: 6

Ingredients

- Skillet stew
- 3-4 tbsp olive oil, divided
- 8 ounces crimini mushrooms, quartered
- 4 vegan italian sausages, cut into 1/4″ slices (368g pkg)
- 1 large yellow onion, diced
- 4 medium carrots, diced
- 2 stalks celery, cut into 1/4″ slices
- 3 cloves garlic, minced
- 1 cup apple cider (can substitute red or white wine)
- 2 tbsp tomato paste
- ¼ cup oil-packed sun-dried tomatoes, chopped
- 2 tsp vegan worcestershire sauce
- 1 tbsp soy sauce
- 1 tbsp brown sugar
- 1 tbsp fresh thyme leaves
- ¼ tsp chili flakes, optional
- 1 tsp smoked paprika, optional
- 15 ounces canned kidney beans, drained and rinsed
- 28 ounces canned diced tomatoes (do not drain)
- ¼ cup all-purpose flour
- 1 cup cold water
- Salt & pepper, to taste
- Potato topping
- 1.3 lbs baby potatoes, cut in 1/4″ slices
- 2 tbsp olive oil
- Course salt

Instructions

1. Preheat the oven to 400°F.

2. Heat 1 tbsp of oil in a 10″ cast-iron skillet over medium-high heat. Once hot, add the mushrooms.

3. Do not salt! Stir occasionally only to prevent burning and for even searing.

4. Once seared on most sides, remove the mushrooms from the skillet and set them aside.

5. In the same skillet, heat 2 tbsp of oil. Lightly sear the sausage slices on both sides. This should take 1-2 minutes per side. Remove the sausage from the skillet.

6. If needed, add 1 tbsp olive oil to the skillet. Reduce the heat to medium. Sauté the onion until translucent. Add the celery, carrots, and garlic to the skillet. Deglaze with the cider, scraping the bottom of the skillet to get all of the flavors into the liquid. Bring to a simmer and reduce the liquid by half.

7. Whisk in the tomato paste, vegan Worcestershire, soy sauce, brown sugar, thyme (and chili flakes and smoked paprika if using).

8. Add the kidney beans, canned tomatoes, and sun-dried tomatoes.

9. Bring things back to a simmer, then add the mushrooms and sausage back in. Simmer for about 5 minutes, or until the volume reduces so you have at least 1/2″ of space above the stew for the potatoes.

10. Whisk the water with the flour until a smooth paste is formed. With the stew simmering, slowly drizzle the paste into the center of the stew and whisk constantly so no lumps form.

11. Stirring constantly, cook until the gravy has thickened. Taste, and add salt and pepper if desired. Turn the heat off.

12. Toss the baby potato slices with olive oil. Layer them over the stew, allowing them to overlap each other by about 1/4″. Sprinkle with coarse salt. Bake for 25-30 minutes or until the potatoes are cooked through.

Nutrition Information

Calories: 463kcal | Carbohydrates: 59g | Protein: 21g | Fat: 17g |

122. Veggie Baked Omelette In A Cast Iron Skillet

Prep Time: 9 Minutes Cook Time: 8 Minutes

Additional Time: 13 Minutes Servings: 8 Servings

Ingredients

- 8 Eggs
- 3 cups Assortment of Veggies
- 2 tbsp Heavy Cream
- 1 tbsp Basil, Oregano, and/or parsley
- 1 tsp Salt
- 1 tsp Pepper
- 2 tbsp Butter
- Grated Cheese

Instructions

1. Preheat the oven to 350 degrees. Preheat cast iron on medium heat.
2. Let the butter melt and add diced vegetables to the sauté for 8 minutes.
3. While veggies are cooking, beat eggs in a bowl, then mix in herbs and cream.
4. Remove cast iron from heat and add 1 tbsp butter.
5. Add egg mixture to cast iron skillet. Stir this mixture in the pan to ensure it mixes.
6. Bake in the oven for 13 minutes.
7. Top with cheese and enjoy!

Nutrition Information

Calories: 362kcal Total Fat: 10gCarbohydrates: 4g| Fiber: 2g| Protein: 8g

123. Seitan Skillet With Peppers And Onions

Prep Time: 5 mins Cook Time: 15 mins

Total Time: 20 mins Servings: 3

Ingredients

- 2 tbsp olive oil, divided
- 1 large onion, chopped
- 1 red bell pepper, chopped
- 8 ozs seitan, sliced thin
- 1 tbsp ketchup
- 1 tbsp soy sauce
- ½ tsp cumin
- ½ tsp garlic powder
- 1 tsp apple vinegar
- A handful of baby spinach

Instructions

1. Heat 1 Tbsp olive oil in a skillet on medium heat. Add the onion, cook for five minutes until it begins to soften.
2. Add the bell pepper to the skillet and cook for another 5 minutes.
3. While the onions and pepper cook, make the sauce in a small bowl. Combine the ketchup, soy sauce, cumin, garlic powder, the remaining Tbsp of olive oil, and champagne vinegar. Whisk together and set aside.
4. After the bell pepper has cooked for 5 minutes, add the seitan to the skillet. Add the sauce, and stir so that the seitan, onions, and peppers are well combined.
5. Cook the seitan for 5 minutes, stirring occasionally, followed by the spinach if using. The dish is ready to serve after 5 minutes of cooking everything together.

Nutrition Facts

Calories: 442kcal Total Fat: 11. Total: Carbohydrate: 15.3g| Protein: 8.7g

124. Summer Veggie Sausage Skillet

Prep Time: 20 minutes Cook Time: 20 minutes

Total Time: 40 minutes Servings: 6

Ingredients

- 4 medium potato, red
- 1 medium onion
- 1 medium bell pepper, red
- 2 clove garlic
- 3 tablespoon olive oil
- 1 pound chicken apple sausage
- 1 medium zucchini
- 1 cup diced mushrooms, portabella
- 1/2 tsp. sea salt
- 1/2 teaspoon black pepper, ground
- 2 Tbsp parsley, fresh

Instructions

1. Rinse and cut each potato into 8-12 pieces Dice onion and pepper. Mince garlic. Place aside, separately.

2. Add 2 Tbsp olive oil to a large skillet over medium. Once hot add potatoes, pepper, and onion.
3. Saute for 6-7 minutes, allowing the potato to soften.
4. Meanwhile, cut zucchini into 1/2 inch thick rounds and then into half-moons. Slice mushrooms. Add zucchini, mushrooms, and garlic to the skillet. Stir to combine, cover, and continue to cook for 2-3 minutes. Stir halfway through cook time.
5. Pour into a bowl, cover, and set aside.
6. Add remaining olive oil to skillet and heat over medium. Slice sausage into thin rounds; 1/2 inch thick. Add to hot skillet and cook for 5-6 minutes. When done, sausage should no longer be pink.
7. Add veggies back to the skillet, season with salt, pepper, and fresh parsley. Stir together and heat through; 2-3 minutes. Serve with fruit.

Nutritional Value

Calories: 482kcal | Carbohydrates: 45g | Protein: 21g | Fat: 23g

125. Vegetarian Sausage Skillet Pizza

Prep Time: 10 Mins Cook Time: 10 Mins

Rising Time: 1 Hr 30 Mins Servings: 3

Ingredients

For The Pizza Dough:

- 180 ml (¾ cup) warm water
- 1 teaspoon active dry yeast
- 225 g (2 cups) plain flour (all-purpose)
- 1 teaspoon sea salt
- 1 teaspoon olive oil
- TOPPINGS (OPTIONAL):
- 2 sausages I used vegan sausages
- 1 Tbsp olive oil
- 100 g (1 cup) sliced mushrooms
- ½ onion thinly sliced
- 1 tsp. thyme leaves
- 1 clove garlic finely chopped
- 2 teaspoons tomato paste
- 1 ball mozzarella cheese

To Cook:

- 2 teaspoons oil

To Serve:

- Rocket / arugula
- Fresh basil

Instructions

1. Pour the water into the bowl of the stand mixer. Sprinkle the yeast over the water, and let it stand for a few minutes until the yeast has dissolved.
2. Insert the dough hook, add the flour and salt to the yeast water and knead with the machine for a few minutes until the dough forms a smooth ball. If the dough is still too sticky, add a Tbsp of flour at a time until it is manageable.
3. Don't add too much or it will affect the result.
4. Pour the water into a large mixing bowl. Sprinkle the yeast over the water, and let it stand for a few minutes until the yeast has dissolved.
5. Add the flour and salt to the bowl of water and stir until it forms a loose dough. Tip the dough onto a lightly floured countertop and knead firmly for 10 minutes or until it's smooth. If the dough is still too sticky, add a Tbsp of flour at a time until it is manageable. Don't add too much or it will affect the result.
6. Put the dough into a large lightly oiled bowl, turn the dough so both sides are covered in oil, and cover tightly with plastic wrap or a tea towel.
7. Allow the dough to rise for 1 ½ hour in a warm place.
8. When you're ready to cook the pizza, divide the dough in half, then on a lightly floured surface shape one of the pieces into a round to fit the bottom of your skillet or baking tray. Pressing rather than rolling makes the pizza crust lighter with more air pockets. Set aside.
9. Cut the sausages into small pieces and cook in a frying pan until browned and cooked through. Slice the mushrooms and onions and cook in another pan with the oil, thyme, and garlic. Set the toppings aside.
10. Heat the oil in an ovenproof frying pan or skillet on the stovetop over medium/high heat and turn on the grill (broiler).
11. Carefully place a disc of dough into the skillet and cook on the stovetop for 1-2 minutes. The dough will puff up and go golden on the underside. Reduce the heat to medium/low and carefully flip the dough over. While

the skillet is still over the heat, add half of the toppings as desired.

12. Continue to cook the pizza for a few minutes and check that the underside of the pizza is golden. When it is move the skillet to the grill (broiler) and heat until the cheese is melted.

13. Transfer to a plate to cool while you continue with the next skillet pizza. Serve topped with the rocket and fresh basil.

Nutritional Value

Calories: 450kcal| Carbohydrates: 63g| Protein: 16g| Fat: 15g|

DESSERT RECIPES

126. Skillet Cookie

Prep Time: 20 minutes Cook Time: 15 minutes

Total Time: 35 minutes Servings: 4 people

Ingredients

- 8 Tbsp. unsalted butter
- 1 1/4 cup All-Purpose Flour
- 1/2 tsp. baking powder
- 1/2 tsp. baking soda
- 1/2 tsp. sea salt
- 1 large egg
- 1/2 cup brown sugar, packed
- 1/4 cup granulated sugar
- 1 Tbsp. milk
- 1 tsp. vanilla extract
- 4 oz. semi-sweet chocolate chunks
- 1/2 cup milk chocolate chips
- 1 Tbsp. softened butter to grease cast iron

Instructions

1. Preheat the oven to 350°F

2. Make the browned butter* and set it aside in a large bowl to cool.

3. While the butter cools, whisk together the flour, baking powder, baking soda, and salt in a medium-sized bowl.

4. Once the browned butter has cooled, whisk in the egg, brown sugar, granulated sugar, vanilla extract, and milk.

5. Stir dry ingredients into wet and then gently fold in the milk chocolate chips and combine.

6. Grease a 10 inch cast iron skillet with softened butter.

7. Spread batter into the skillet evenly using a rubber spatula. Top with chocolate chunks. Bake for ~15-17 minutes or until the edges are slightly browned. Oven times may vary.

8. Cool for a few minutes before digging in, if you can wait! Serve with vanilla bean ice cream.

Nutritional Value

Calories: 675kcal | Carbohydrates: 87g | Protein: 7g | Fat: 35g |

127. Gooey Texas Chocolate Sheet Cake Skillet

Prep Time: 10 minutes Cook Time: 35 minutes

Total Time: 45 minutes Servings: 4

Ingredients

- 8 ounces butter chopped (2 sticks)
- 1 cup water
- 4 Tbsp unsweetened cocoa powder
- 2 cups sugar
- 2 cups all-purpose flour
- 1 tsp baking soda
- 1/2 tsp salt
- 1/2 cup sour cream
- 2 eggs
- 1 tsp vanilla
- 6 Tbsp milk
- 3 Tbsp unsweetened cocoa powder
- 4 ounces butter chopped (1 stick)
- 3 3/4 cup powdered sugar
- 3/4 cup pecan bits

Instructions

1. Preheat oven to 350 F

2. Spray a medium skillet (I used a 10 inch) with nonstick spray.

3. In a medium saucepan, heat the water, cocoa, and butter over medium heat. Bring to a boil and then remove from the heat.

4. Meanwhile, in a large bowl, combine flour, sugar, baking soda, and salt. Stir to combine.

5. In a separate small bowl, lightly whisk the eggs. Whisk in the sour cream and vanilla and combine fully. Pour egg mixture over flour mixture and use a wooden spoon to stir until fully combined.
6. Pour chocolate mixture over flour batter and use a whisk or hand mixer to fully combine until fully smooth.
7. Pour mixture into skillet.
8. Bake for 30-35 minutes or until almost cooked through. The cake should no longer jiggle in the middle but a toothpick inserted in the middle may still have a bit of chocolate on it. If you prefer your cake fully cooked, cook until the toothpick comes out completely clean, about 35-40 minutes. (NOTE: This also depends on the size of your skillet. If you use a larger skillet, cook times will be less. It's great to check this recipe halfway through to monitor its doneness)
9. After removing the cake from the oven, prepare your frosting.
10. In a medium saucepan over medium heat, combine the milk, cocoa, and butter. Bring to a boil.
11. Remove from the heat and add the powdered sugar. Use a hand mixer to beat the icing until fully smooth.
12. Stir in the pecan bits with a spoon.
13. Pour the icing over the warm cake and allow to cool another 10 minutes.
14. Serve garnished with ice cream and share with all of your friends! The more the merrier.

Nutrition Information

Calories: 893kcal| Carbohydrates: 133g| Protein: 6g| Fat: 39g|

128. Cinnamon Roll Skillet Cake

Prep Time: 10 Mins Cook Time: 30 Mins

Total Time: 40 Mins Servings: 4

Ingredients

Cake Ingredients:

- 1 ½ cups all-purpose flour or gluten-free substitute
- ⅓ cup sugar
- 2 tsp.s baking powder
- teaspoon salt
- ¾ cup milk or dairy-free alternative
- 1 egg
- ¼ cup unsalted butter melted (or dairy-free substitute)
- 1 tsp. vanilla extract
- ¼ cup unsalted butter melted
- ¼ cup brown sugar packed
- 1 teaspoon ground cinnamon
- 1 cup powdered sugar
- 1-2 Tbsp milk
- 1 teaspoon vanilla extract

Instructions

1. Preheat oven to 350 degrees F. Grease a 9" cast iron skillet and set aside.
2. In a large mixing bowl, add flour, sugar, baking powder, and salt. Stir to combine.
3. Add milk, egg, melted butter, and vanilla extract to the dry ingredients. Stir well to incorporate. Pour cake batter into prepared skillet. Use the handle of a mixing spoon to poke holes throughout the cake.
4. In a small bowl, add cinnamon sugar topping ingredients and stir to combine. Spoon the topping onto the cake - be sure to fill the holes. Take a butter knife and swirl the cinnamon sugar topping into the cake batter. Bake in preheated oven for 27-30 minutes. Remove from oven and allow the cake to cool for 10 minutes.
5. While the cake is cooling, combine the vanilla icing drizzle ingredients in a small bowl. Use a spoon to drizzle over the top of the cake. Slice and serve warm.

Nutritional Value

Carbohydrates: 8g | Protein: 18g | Fat: 12g | Saturated Fat: 7g |

129. The Best Chocolate Chip Skillet Cookie

Prep Time: 20 Mins Cook Time: 22 Mins

Total Time: 42 Mins Servings: 4

Ingredients

- 10 tablespoon unsalted butter
- ⅓ cup granulated sugar
- ⅔ cup light brown sugar
- 1 tsp. vanilla extract
- 1 large egg
- 1¾ cups all-purpose flour

- ½ teaspoon baking soda
- ¼ teaspoon salt
- ¾ cup chocolate chunks

Instructions

1. Heat oven to 350°F. In a 10-inch ovenproof skillet (such as a cast-iron skillet), melt butter over medium-low heat and remove the pan from the stove. Stir in granulated sugar, brown sugar, and vanilla and cool about 5 min.
2. Whisk the egg into the pan until blended. Add flour, baking soda, and salt and stir until smooth. Quickly stir in chocolate chunks.
3. Press the dough into the skillet in an even layer. Bake until the surface is golden but the center is still soft, 18 to 22 minutes.

Nutritional Value

Calories: 482kcal Carbohydrates: 37g| Protein: 3g| Fat: 14g|

130. Skillet Chocolate Chip Cookie

Prep Time: 10 Mins Cook Time: 20 Mins

Total Time: 30 Mins Servings: 4

Ingredients

- 3/4 cup unsalted butter, melted
- 1 cup packed brown sugar
- 1/2 cup granulated sugar
- 1 large egg
- 1 egg yolk
- 2 tsp.s pure vanilla extract
- 2 cups all-purpose flour
- 1 teaspoon cornstarch
- 3/4 teaspoon baking soda
- 1/2 teaspoon sea salt
- 1 cup chocolate chips
- Flaky sea salt, for sprinkling

Instructions

1. Preheat oven to 350° F. Grease a 12-inch cast-iron skillet and set aside.
2. In a large bowl, combine melted butter, brown sugar, and granulated sugar.
3. Stir until smooth.
4. Add the egg, egg yolk, and vanilla and mix until combined.
5. Add the flour, cornstarch, baking soda, and salt. Stir until flour disappears. Stir in the chocolate chips.
6. Spread batter evenly in prepared cast iron skillet.
7. Sprinkle the top with a little sea salt. Bake for 20-22 minutes or until golden brown.
8. Don't overbake, you want the cookie to be slightly gooey.
9. Remove from oven and let cool on a wire cooling rack for 10-15 minutes. Serve with ice cream, if desired.

Nutrition Value

Calories: 441kcal| Carbohydrates: 63g| Protein: 4g| Fat: 19g|

131. Cast Iron Skillet Cake

Prep Time: 25 minutes Cook Time: 30 minutes

Total Time: 55 minutes Servings: 12

Ingredients

Buttermilk Skillet Cake

- 2 cups all-purpose flour
- 1 teaspoon baking powder
- ½ tsp. baking soda
- ½ teaspoon kosher salt
- 8 Tbsp butter softened
- 1¼ cups sugar
- 2 eggs + 1 egg yolk room temperature
- 2 teaspoon vanilla
- 1 cup buttermilk room temperature
- 1 cup brown sugar
- ¾ cup (1½ sticks) butter
- ⅓ cup cream
- ⅛ teaspoon kosher salt
- 1 teaspoon vanilla
- 1¼ cups pecans chopped

Instructions

Skillet Cake

1. Preheat oven to 375°F and spray a 12 inch cast iron skillet with non-stick baking spray.

2. In a small bowl, whisk together the flour, baking soda, baking powder, and salt. Set aside.
3. In a stand mixer fitted with the paddle attachment, cream the butter and sugar together on medium speed until light and fluffy, about 3 minutes.
4. Add the eggs and egg yolk one at a time, beating for 1 minute between each addition and scraping the sides of the bowl occasionally. Add the vanilla and mix until just combined.
5. Add half the dry mixture and mix at low speed until just combined. Add the buttermilk and mix until mostly combined. Then add remaining dry ingredients and mix until just combined. The batter will be thick.
6. Pour the batter into the prepared skillet and spread evenly to the edges. Bake for 25-35 minutes until golden brown and a toothpick inserted in the middle comes out clean. Don't overbake.

Praline Sauce

7. Combine the brown sugar, butter, cream, and salt in a small saucepan. Cook over medium-low heat until melted.
8. Bring the mixture to a soft boil for 3-5 minutes, stirring often. The sugar should be dissolved.
9. Remove from the heat and mix in the vanilla and pecans. Let cool for 15-20 minutes to thicken while the cake finishes baking.

Assemble

10. Remove cake from the oven and cool for 5 minutes. Pour warm praline sauce on warm cake and spread with a spatula to the edges. Allow to cool for 10 minutes, then serve warm! Top with vanilla ice cream if desired.

Storage And Freezing

11. Store in an air-tight container or cake plate at room temperature for 1-2 days. Freeze leftover slices in an air-tight container or wrap individually for up to 3 months. Thaw at room temperature and reheat gently in the microwave.

Nutritional Value

Calories: 519kcal | Carbohydrates: 58g | Protein: 5g | Fat: 31g |

132. Cast Iron Skillet Blueberry Cobbler

Prep Time: 10 Minutes Cook Time: 40 Minutes

Total Time: 50 Minutes Servings: 1

Ingredients

- 2 cups fresh blueberries
- 1 stick butter
- 1 1/2 cups sugar
- 1 tsp lemon zest
- 1 cup milk
- 1 cup self-rising flour
- 1 tsp cinnamon

Instructions

1. Preheat oven to 350
2. Melt butter in your cast iron skillet
3. Add 1/2 cup sugar, lemon zest, and blueberries
4. on low heat cook until sugar dissolves and slightly thickens about 3 minutes.
5. In a separate bowl mix together flour, cinnamon, 1 cup sugar, and milk.
6. blend until smooth.
7. Pour batter over the blueberry mix.
8. bake for 40 minutes or until the top is golden brown.
9. optional sprinkle with sugar when done.

Nutrition Information

Calories: 482kcal Total Fat: 9g|| Carbohydrates: 44g| Protein: 2g

133. Grilled Triple Berry Crisp In A Cast Iron Skillet

Prep Time: 5 minutes Cook Time: 45 minutes

Total Time: 50 minutes Servings: 8

Ingredients

- 16 ounces fresh strawberries sliced

- 6 ounces fresh blackberries
- 1 pint fresh blueberries
- 1/4 cup sugar
- 2 tsp.s lemon zest
- 1/2 teaspoon vanilla
- 1/4 tsp. cinnamon
- 1 cup all-purpose flour
- 1/2 cup sugar
- 1/4 cup room temperature butter
- 1/2 teaspoon salt
- 1/4 tsp. cinnamon

Instructions

Berry Filling

1. Stir together berry filling ingredients in a 9 or 10" cast iron skillet.
2. Crisp Topping
3. Stir together flour, sugar, and salt in a small mixing bowl.
4. Using a fork or a pastry cutter, cut butter into dry ingredients until you have coarse crumbs.
5. Spread evenly over the berry mixture.
6. Sprinkle the top with cinnamon.
7. Bake on indirect heat in a covered grill at medium-low heat, approximately 300 degrees, for 45 minutes or until the berries are bubbling at the edges and the crisp is golden brown.
8. Serve warm with whipped cream or vanilla bean ice cream.

Nutritional Value

Calories: 242kcal | Carbohydrates: 45g | Protein: 2g | Fat: 6g |

134. Cast-Iron Skillet French Apple Cake

Prep Time: 20 mins Cook Time: 55 mins

Total Time: 1 hr 15 mins Servings: 8 servings

Ingredients

- 1 stick (120 g) unsalted butter, melted
- 1 ¼ pound (625 g) Gala or Honeycrisp apples, 4 or 5 small
- 1 cup (140 g) all-purpose flour
- ¾ tsp. baking powder
- ½ tsp. fine sea salt
- 2 eggs
- ¾ cup (180 g) granulated sugar
- 3 Tbsp (45 ml) whiskey, bourbon, Cognac, or apple brandy
- ½ teaspoon vanilla extract
- ⅓ cup (75 ml) buttermilk
- 2 Tbsp (30 g) turbinado sugar

Instructions

1. Preheat oven to 350 degrees (175C)
2. Brush a 9 or 10-inch cast-iron skillet with enough of the melted butter (about 1 tablespoon) to lightly coat it on the bottom and sides.
3. Core the apples and peel all but one. Slice the unpeeled apple into half moons about ¼-inch thick. Cut the remaining apples into ½-inch chunks.
4. Whisk the flour, baking powder, and salt together in a mixing bowl.
5. Lightly beat the eggs in another bowl with the sugar just until foamy (an immersion blender is great for this task). Stir in the whiskey, vanilla, and buttermilk.
6. Pour half of the egg mixture over the flour mixture and fold briefly. Pour in the remaining butter and stir. Add the remaining egg mixture and stir until no flour is visible. Add the chopped apples and stir gently to blend.
7. Spoon the batter into the skillet. Arrange the sliced apples on the top, then sprinkle with the turbinado sugar.
8. Bake until the cake springs back when poked in the center, and the edges are golden brown, 55-60 minutes. Cool 10 minutes. Dust with powdered sugar and serve warm or at room temperature.

Nutritional Value

Calories: 316kcal | Carbohydrates: 44g | Protein: 4g | Fat: 13g

135. Skillet Chocolate Chip Cookie

Prep Time: 10 Minutes Cook Time: 20 Minutes

Total Time: 30 Minutes Servings: 8 Large Slices

Ingredients

- 6 Tbsp butter, softened
- ⅓ cup packed light brown sugar

- ½ cup granulated sugar
- 1 large egg
- 1 teaspoon vanilla extract
- 1 cup all-purpose flour
- ½ tsp. baking soda
- ¼ teaspoon salt
- 1 cup semi-sweet chocolate chips

Instructions

1. Preheat the oven to 350 degrees.
2. Stir together the flour, salt, and baking soda, set aside.
3. In another bowl, using a wooden spoon, combine the sugars and the butter until well blended.
4. Stir in the egg and the vanilla until blended. Stir in the flour mixture. Stir in the chocolate chips.
5. Spread evenly into a 10-inch cast-iron skillet. Bake for 20 to 25 minutes or until the center is just set. Allow cooling for at least 10 minutes before cutting.

Nutrition Information

Calories: 447kcal Total Fat: 16g| Carbohydrates: 46g | Protein: 3g

136. Skillet Berry Crumble

Prep Time: 15 mins Cook Time: 45 mins

Servings: 8

Ingredients

- Berry Base
- 5 cups fresh berries
- 1 zest of orange
- 1/4 cup fresh-squeezed orange juice
- 1/2 cup granulated sugar
- 1/2 cup all-purpose flour
- 1 tablespoon cornstarch
- 1/2 tsp. salt
- Crumble Topping
- 1 cup all-purpose flour
- 1 cup oatmeal
- 1/2 cup granulated sugar
- 1/2 teaspoon salt
- 1 teaspoon cinnamon
- 1 1/2 sticks cold butter (cut into small cubes)

Instructions

1. Preheat oven to 375°F.
2. In a mixing bowl, toss together berries, orange zest and juice, sugar, flour, cornstarch, and salt. Smooth berry into an even layer. Transfer berry mixture to a 10 inch cast iron skillet.
3. Spread topping evenly on top of the berry mixture with a spatula.
4. Bake for 40 to 45 minutes until berry juices are bubbling
5. Serve warm with ice cream

Nutritional Value

Calories: 482kcal | Carbohydrates: 41g | Protein: 2g | Fat: 10g |

137. Mini Fruit Cobblers

Prep Time: 8 min Cook Time: 22 min

Ready in 30 min

Ingredients

- 1 can (21 oz. /595 g) any flavor pie filling (about 2 cups/500 mL)
- ½ cup (125 mL) self-rising flour
- ½ cup (125 mL) heavy whipping cream
- Ground cinnamon and sugar, to taste
- Vanilla ice cream or whipped cream (optional)

Instructions

1. Preheat oven to 400°F (200°C). Pour the pie filling in equal parts into two 5.5" (14-cm) Cast Iron Skillets.
2. In a medium bowl, combine the flour and heavy whipping cream. Use the Medium Scoop to add dough to each skillet. If desired, sprinkle with cinnamon and sugar.
3. Bake for 20 minutes or until the biscuit dough is lightly browned.
4. Remove from the oven; let stand 5 minutes and serve with vanilla ice cream or whipped cream, if desired.

Nutrients Value

Calories: 382kcal Total Fat: 22g | Carbohydrate: 157g| Protein: 6g

138. Mini Skillet Apple Crisps

Prep Time: 15 min Cook Time: 45 min

Total Time: 1 hour Servings: 4

Ingredients

- 5 Honeycrisp or Granny Smith apples (peeled, cored, and thinly sliced)
- 1/2 teaspoon cinnamon
- 1/4 tsp. ground ginger
- 1 Tbsp brown sugar
- Juice from 1/2 lemon
- 1 Tbsp flour

For The Crisp Topping:

- 1 cup flour
- 1/2 cup sugar
- 1 tsp. cinnamon
- 1/2 teaspoon ground nutmeg
- 1/4 tsp. salt
- 1 stick butter (cold, cut into 6 pieces)
- 4 pats of butter
- Vanilla ice cream for serving

Instructions

1. Preheat the oven to 350 degrees.
2. Place peeled, cored, and thinly sliced apples in a large mixing bowl. Add to the apples the cinnamon, ginger, brown sugar, lemon juice, and flour. Toss well to coat. Set aside.
3. In a food processor fitted with the steel blade, place the flour, sugar, cinnamon, nutmeg, and salt and mix briefly until thoroughly combined. Add in the cut pieces of butter until it forms a coarse paste.
4. Melt a pat of butter into four mini cast iron skillets. Add a layer of the apple mixture into each skillet and top each with the crisp topping. Bake in the oven for 45 to 50 minutes until apples are tender. (Cover the tops with foil if the topping starts to burn.)
5. Remove from the oven and let cool slightly (3 min. tops) and top each apple crisp with a scoop of vanilla ice cream.

Nutritional Value

Calories: 500| Fat: 23.5g| Carbohydrates: 71.4g| Protein: 4.1g

139. Cast Iron Skillet Brownies

Servings: 6-8 Servings Prep Time: 10 Minutes

Cook Time: 35 Minutes Servings: 4

Ingredients

- 1 cup butter, melted
- 2 cups sugar
- 3 eggs
- 1 tsp vanilla extract
- 2 tbsp espresso or very strong coffee (can substitute with water if you prefer)
- 2/3 cup cocoa powder, preferably dutch
- 1 cup all-purpose flour
- 1/4 tsp salt
- 1/2 tsp baking powder
- Powdered sugar, for dusting (optional)

Instructions

1. Preheat the oven to 350F.
2. In a medium mixing bowl, combine the melted butter and sugar until it's thoroughly mixed. Add the eggs and vanilla and mix it again until it's thoroughly mixed.
3. Mix the dry ingredients in another bowl, then add it to the wet ingredients and mix just until it's combined.
4. Pour the mixture into a large cast-iron skillet (or a 13×9 pan) and bake for 30-35 minutes or until a toothpick inserted into the center comes out with just a few crumbs.
5. Cool the brownies to room temperature then dust with the powdered sugar. Serve with vanilla ice cream, salted caramel sauce, hot fudge, and/or chopped pecans, if desired.

Nutrition Information

Calories: 569| Total Fat: 26g| Carbohydrates: 81g| Protein: 6g

140. Brown Butter Peach Cast Iron Skillet Cake

Prep Time: 10 minutes Cook Time: 30 minutes

Total Time: 40 minutes Servings: 8 slices

Ingredients

- 1 cupcake flour, substitute all-purpose flour
- ¾ cup brown sugar
- 1 ½ teaspoons baking powder
- ½ tsp. cinnamon
- ¼ teaspoon salt
- 1 cup whole milk
- 1 teaspoon vanilla extract
- ½ cup unsalted butter
- 4 large fresh peaches, sliced
- Powdered sugar, for dusting

Instructions

1. Preheat oven to 350°F.
2. Whisk together the flour, brown sugar, baking powder, cinnamon, and salt in a medium-sized bowl. Add in the milk and vanilla and mix until fully combined and smooth.
3. Melt the butter in a 10-inch cast-iron skillet over medium heat (this both preheats and greases the pan).
4. Once melted stir frequently and watch closely for the formation of brown specs on the bottom of the pan.
5. First, the batter will get thick and foamy. Then it will start to bubble rapidly. Don't stop stirring the butter. After a few minutes, the butter will start to turn a golden brown color and you'll start to see those brown specs on the bottom of the pan. It will smell intensely buttery, nutty, and rich.
6. Once you see the brown specs, remove from the heat and immediately pour into the cake batter (it's okay if a little butter stays behind) and stir to combine.
7. Pour the batter into the hot greased pan and smooth into an even layer. Then top with the sliced peaches.
8. Bake the skillet cake at 350°F for 30-40 minutes or until the batter is fully set and the top is browned.
9. Dust the peach skillet cake with powdered sugar and serve warm with whipped cream or vanilla ice cream!

Nutritional Value

Calories: 382kcal Carbohydrates: 33g | Protein: 3g | Fat: 13g |

141. Double Chocolate Skillet Brownies

Prep Time: 10 Minutes Cook Time: 30 Minutes

Total Time: 40 Minutes Servings: 8-12

Ingredients

- 1 Cup of flour
- 1/2 Cup of cocoa powder
- 1/2 Cup of granulated sugar
- 1/2 Cup of brown sugar
- 1/2 Tsp salt
- 1 Tbsp of vanilla
- 1 stick of butter (1/2 cup), melted
- 3 Eggs
- 1 Cup of chocolate chips

Instructions

1. Combine all dry ingredients in a large mixing bowl. Mix well.
2. Add melted butter, eggs, and vanilla and mix with a hand mixer just until everything is well incorporated.
3. Add Chocolate chips and give a quick swirl to mix into the batter.
4. Transfer to a 10" Cast iron skillet.
5. Bake at 350°F for 30 minutes.

Nutrition Information

Calories: 271| Total Fat: 14g| Carbohydrates: 35g| Protein: 4g

142. Mini Berry Skillet Cake

Prep Time: 5 Minutes Cook Time: 22 Minutes

Total Time: 27 Minutes Servings: 1 Mini Skillet Cake

Ingredients

- 2 Tbsp White Whole Wheat Flour
- 1 tablespoon plus 1/2 teaspoon Brown Sugar, divided
- 1/8 teaspoon Baking Powder
- Pinch of Fine Sea Salt
- 2 Tbsp Milk, (use non-dairy for vegan)
- 1/8 tsp. Vanilla Extract
- 1 Tbsp Grapeseed Oil (plus more for oiling the pan)

• 1 tsp. Mini Semi-Sweet Chocolate Chips, (use non-dairy for vegan)
• 1/4 cup Frozen Berries, (do not thaw)
• Optional Toppings
• Ice cream, melted chocolate chips, whipped cream, yogurt

Instructions

1. Adjust your toaster oven's cooking rack to the bottom position, select the BAKE setting, and preheat to 350°F.
2. Lightly oil a 3.5 inch cast iron skillet, set aside.
3. In a small bowl whisk together the flour, 1 Tbsp brown sugar, the baking powder, and salt until no clumps remain.
4. Whisk in the milk, vanilla, and oil until smooth. Stir in the mini chocolate chips.
5. Pour batter into the prepared skillet. Top with frozen berries and sprinkle the remaining 1/2 teaspoon of brown sugar over the fruit.
6. Bake until the cake is lightly golden, browned around the edges, and the fruit is bubbly for about 20 to 24 minutes.
7. Allow the cake to cool until you can safely touch the skillet. Then add your favorite toppings and dig in!

Nutrition Information

Calories: 269| Total Fat: 15.3g| Carbohydrates: 31.6g| | Protein: 3.6g

143. Mini Skillet Brownie

Prep Time: 5 mins Cook Time: 20 mins

Total Time: 25 mins Servings: 4

Ingredients

• ¼ cup all-purpose flour 35g plain flour
• 1 Tbsp unsweetened cocoa powder
• ¼ tsp. salt
• ⅛ tsp. cinnamon
• ¼ cup semi-sweet chocolate chips 44g
• 4 Tbsp unsalted butter 55g
• ¼ cup sugar 50g
• 1 egg
• ¼ teaspoon vanilla extract
• 1 Tbsp bittersweet chocolate chips

Instructions

1. Preheat the oven to 350F/180C. Lightly butter the inside of a 6 ½ in cast iron skillet (16.5cm frying pan).
2. Whisk together the flour, cocoa powder, salt, and cinnamon and set aside.
3. Melt the butter and ¼ cup chocolate chips together in a heatproof bowl. You can either do this in short bursts of around 20-30 seconds in the microwave, stirring in between, until almost melted, or else in a double broiler. Remove from heat once almost melted and stir to melt the last little bit.
4. Stir the sugar into the chocolate mixture until well combined. Add the vanilla and egg and stir/whisk to mix through. Make sure you do this relatively quickly so the egg doesn't cook as bits of egg.
5. Gradually add the flour mixture and fold in, then fold in the remaining chocolate chips. Once it's all mixed in, pour into the prepared skillet. Spread the mixture to the edges and smooth the top.
6. Bake the brownie in the oven for approximately 18-20 minutes until it is dry on top and gently crisp around the edges. You can test with a skewer in the middle which should come out clean (apart from any chocolate if you catch a chip). Best served warm but you can also serve at room temperature.

Nutritional Value

Calories: 564kcal | Carbohydrates: 56g | Protein: 7g | Fat: 36g |

144. Skillet Cookie

Prep Time: 10 Minutes Cook Time: 25 Minutes

Total Time: 35 Minutes Servings: 8

Ingredients

• 2 ½ cups all-purpose flour
• 1 tsp. baking powder
• 3/4 teaspoon salt
• 1/4 tsp. baking soda
• 1 cup unsalted butter, softened
• 3/4 cup granulated sugar
• 3/4 cup light brown sugar, firmly packed
• 2 large eggs, room temperature
• 2 teaspoons vanilla extract

• 1 ½ cups chocolate chips, semi-sweet, dark or milk

Instructions

1. Preheat the oven to 350 degrees F.
2. In a small bowl, whisk together flour, baking powder, salt, and baking soda. Set aside.
3. In a large bowl, cream together butter and sugars, beating until light and fluffy.
4. Beat in eggs, one at a time, until smooth. Add vanilla & mix in.
5. Gradually add flour mixture to wet mixture, scraping down the sides of the bowl after each addition.
6. Stir in chocolate chips, reserving a handful.
7. Spread the dough evenly in a 10-inch cast-iron skillet. Scatter the reserved chocolate chips on top.
8. Bake for about 25-30 minutes, until the center is cooked through and a toothpick inserted in the center comes out clean.
9. Remove from the oven and cool slightly.
10. Serve warm with vanilla ice cream and toppings if desired.

Nutritional Value

Calories: 516kcal | Carbohydrates: 69g | Protein: 6g | Fat: 24g

145. Skillet Apple Crisp

Prep Time: 10 minutes Cook Time: 40 minutes

Total Time: 50 minutes Servings: 8

Ingredients

- Apple Crisp Filling
- 6 granny smith apples
- 1/4 cup light brown sugar (lightly packed)
- 1/4 cup granulated white sugar
- 2 tbsp unsalted butter if butter is salted, omit the extra salt
- 2 tsp pumpkin pie spice (or equal parts, cinnamon, nutmeg, clove)
- 1 tbsp fresh lemon juice
- 1/4 tsp kosher salt

Apple Crisp Topping

- 1 cup all-purpose flour
- 1 cup old-fashioned oats
- 1/3 cup light brown sugar (packed)
- 1/2 cup chopped pecans (optional)
- 1/4 tsp kosher salt
- 1/2 cup unsalted butter (room temp or melted) if butter is salted, omit the extra salt

Instructions

1. Apple Crisp Filling
2. Preheat oven to 350 degrees (set rack in the center).
3. Peel, core, and slice apples.
4. In a large bowl, combine sliced apples, brown sugar, white sugar, pumpkin pie spice, salt, lemon juice, and melted butter. Mix well.
5. Pour apple mixture into cast iron skillet.
6. Apple Crisp Topping
7. In a large bowl, combine flour, oats, brown sugar, pecan, and salt. Mix well.
8. Add melted butter. Hand mix until crumbs form.
9. Evenly sprinkle apple crisp crumble topping over apples in skillet.
10. Bake cast iron skillet apple crisp in the oven for approximately 40 to 50 minutes.
11. Serve warm topped with vanilla ice cream and caramel sauce (optional).

Nutritional Value

Calories: 423kcal | Carbohydrates: 61g | Protein: 4g | Fat: 20g |

146. Skillet Apple Crisp (Alternative Version)

Prep Time: 10 mins Cook Time: 40 mins

Resting Time: 30 mins Servings: 6 Servings

Ingredients

Filling

- 6 medium apples peeled, cored, and cut into small pieces
- 3 Tbsp unsalted butter
- ⅓ cup brown sugar
- 2 teaspoons ground cinnamon
- ⅛ tsp. kosher salt

Topping

- 1 ¼ cup old fashioned oats
- 2 Tbsp all-purpose flour
- 5 Tbsp cold unsalted butter cut into 5 pieces
- ⅓ cup brown sugar
- ⅛ teaspoon kosher salt
- Sprinkle of ground cinnamon

Instructions

1. Preheat the oven to 350 F.
2. Add cut-up, peeled, and cored apple slices to a large mixing bowl and set aside.
3. Preheat a 10 inch cast iron skillet over medium-low heat and melt the butter for the filling.
4. Once the butter is melted, whisk in brown sugar, cinnamon, and salt.
5. Pour the butter mixture over the apples in the mixing bowl and toss until the apples are well coated.
6. Add the apples and butter mixture back into the skillet and turn the heat up to medium. Stir occasionally while it cooks for 5 minutes until the apples begin to soften. Remove the pan from the heat, but keep the apple mixture in it.
7. After the apples are partially cooked, cut the 5 Tbsp of butter into 5 separate pieces.
8. In a medium mixing bowl, add all the toppings EXCEPT the ground cinnamon. Combine ingredients using either your hands or a pastry cutter. It is okay to have small lumps of butter throughout the mixture.
9. Top the apples in the skillet with the topping evenly and sprinkle on the cinnamon. Place in the oven.
10. Cook for 35-40 minutes, until the apples are tender, slightly bubbling and the topping is crunchy.
11. Allow to rest and cool at room temperature for about 30 minutes before serving.

Nutritional Value

Calories: 689kcal | Carbohydrates: 36.8g | Protein: 70.8g | Fat: 28.2g

147. Chocolate Chip Cookie

Prep Time: 10 Mins Cook Time: 35 Mins

Total Time: 30 Mins Servings: 8

Ingredients

- 1 cup (2 sticks) unsalted butter, at room temp, plus more for greasing skillet
- 3 cups all-purpose flour
- 1/2 teaspoon kosher salt
- 1 Tbsp baking powder
- 1 1/4 cups sugar
- 1/2 cup packed light brown sugar
- 3 large eggs, at room temp
- 2 tsp.s vanilla extract
- 2 cups semisweet chocolate chips or chunks
- 1 tsp. flaky sea salt (optional)

Instructions

1. Preheat the oven to 350°F and grease a 12-inch cast-iron skillet with butter.
2. In a medium mixing bowl, whisk together the flour, baking powder, and salt. Set the bowl aside.
3. In a stand mixer fitted with the paddle attachment, cream together 1 cup (2 sticks) unsalted butter with the sugar and light brown sugar.
4. Add eggs, one at a time, until mixed in, then add the vanilla extract and beat until combined.
5. Add the flour mixture into the stand mixer and mix just until the dough comes together then beat in the chocolate until combined.
6. Scrape the dough into the skillet, then sprinkle it with the sea salt.
7. Bake the cookie for 30 to 35 minutes until it's barely cooked in the center.

8. Remove it from the oven and allow it to cool for 10 minutes before serving topped with ice cream (optional).

Nutritional Value

Calories: 482kcal Carbohydrates: 31g | Protein: 17g | Fat: 30g |

148. Peach Cobbler In A Cast-Iron Skillet

Prep Time: 15 Minutes Cook Time: 40 Minutes

Total Time: 55 Minutes Servings: 2

Ingredients

- 2 cups sliced peaches (I used [url undefined]frozen peaches[/url] from last summer's bounty)
- 1/2 cup sugar
- 1/4 cup flour
- 1/2 cup unsalted butter
- 3/4 cup all-purpose flour
- 3/4 cup sugar
- 2 teaspoons baking powder
- 1/4 tsp. salt
- 3/4 cup milk

Instructions

1. Pre-heat oven to 375*F.
2. Places sliced peaches in a large bowl. Sprinkle with 1/2 cup of sugar and flour. Stir to coat peaches and set aside.
3. In a separate bowl, combine flour, 3/4 cup sugar, baking powder, salt, and milk, set aside.
4. Over low heat, melt butter in a cast-iron skillet.
5. Pour the batter over the melted butter - Do not stir into the butter.
6. Pour the peaches over the batter - again, do not stir.
7. Bake for 35 to 40 minutes, until crust is light brown and puffy.
8. Remove from oven and allow to cool slightly before serving.

9. Serve warm with vanilla ice cream or fresh whipped cream.

Nutritional Value

Calories: 475kcal Carbohydrates: 11g | Protein: 17g | Fat: 17g |

149. Cast Iron Skillet Brownies

Prep Time: 15 Mins Cook Time: 25 Mins

Total Time: 40 Minutes Servings: 8 Wedges

Ingredients

Dry Ingredients

- 1/2 cup granulated sugar (I used Turbinado)
- 1/3 cup cocoa (I used raw cacao)
- 1/2 cup flour (I used all-purpose einkorn)
- 1/4 tsp salt
- 1/4 tsp baking powder
- 1/2 cup add-ins: chocolate chips, chopped walnuts, chopped pecans, caramel pieces (optional)

Wet Ingredients

- 2 eggs
- 8 Tbsp (1 stick) butter, melted
- 1 tsp vanilla extract

Instructions

1. Preheat cast-iron skillet for 10 full minutes.
2. Meanwhile, combine butter, chocolate chips, and cocoa in a medium bowl and mash together with a large spoon.
3. In a separate small bowl, combine eggs, vanilla, and sugar. Mix to combine well.
4. Add egg mixture to the chocolate and mix well, ensuring everything is well combined.
5. Add flour, baking powder, and salt to the batter and stir until just combined.
6. When the cast-iron skillet is hot, remove from heat and pour in batter. Cover with aluminum foil and place something heavy on top (i.e. cookie sheet, another pan inverted, lid, etc.).
7. Allow brownie to sit undisturbed for 20 minutes. Test doneness with a knife inserted until just barely clean. Cook over the open fire or on a stove for another 5 minutes if needed, but be careful to not let the pan get too hot otherwise the bottom will burn.
8. Allow cooling slightly before serving directly from the skillet.

Nutritional Value

Calories: 382kcal Carbohydrates: 38g| Protein: 38g| Fat: 13g|

150. Chocolate Chip Skillet Cookie

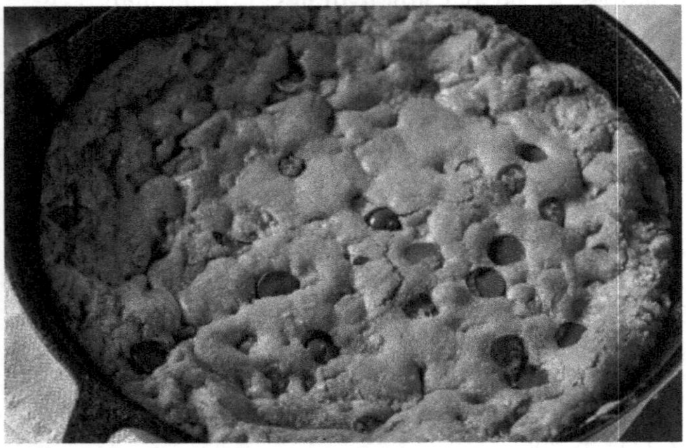

Prep Time: 20 mins Cook Time: 26 mins

Total Time: 46 mins Servings: 6

Ingredients

- 1 cup Butter
- 1 cup Brown Sugar
- 1/2 cup Sugar
- 2 Eggs
- 1 tsp. Vanilla
- 2 cups + 2 Tbsp Flour
- 1 teaspoon Baking Soda
- 1/2 teaspoon salt
- 3/4 cup Milk Chocolate Chunks
- 3/4 cup Semi-sweet Chocolate Chips
- Vanilla Bean Ice Cream

Instructions

1. Preheat oven to 325 degrees.
2. In a 10 or 12 inches cast iron skillet, melt butter over medium heat stirring often, until it starts to bubble and is completely melted. Turn heat to low and add sugar and brown sugar, stirring well. Keep stirring until smooth and glossy.
3. Chill for 10-15 minutes (you don't want to add the eggs now or you will have scrambled eggs).
4. Remove from refrigerator or freezer and add eggs and vanilla and stir well.
5. Stir in flour, baking soda, and salt.
6. Mix in chocolate and stir to combine. *check to see if the dough is at room temperature before adding chocolate to prevent melting.
7. Bake at 325 degrees for 26 - 33 or until the edges are lightly golden brown. *The inside will still be slightly gooey and that's the way it's meant to be. If the edges get too brown, Place some foil over the edges. The smaller the pan, the thicker the dough which means a longer cooking time.
8. Top with vanilla bean ice cream and eat warm.

Nutritional Value

Calories: 262kcal Total Fat: 24g| Carbohydrates: 29g| Protein: 27g

CPSIA information can be obtained
at www.ICGtesting.com
Printed in the USA
LVHW060342230222
711789LV00006B/259

9 781801 886307